Evaluating Psychological Information

Sharpening Your
Critical Thinking Skills
Third Edition

James Bell
Howard Community College

Allyn & Bacon
Boston • London • Toronto • Sydney • Tokyo • Singapore

Contents

Preface

Psychological information provided to the public is often incorrect, incomplete and misleading. The four step procedure presented in this book is useful to separate research from opinions and reliable evidence from propaganda.

Some people believe anything in print. Some ignore all evidence. Both approaches place little emphasis on critical thinking and require little effort from the reader. This book is different from textbooks that teach only the facts and theories of psychology.

> **The purpose of this book is to provide you with the intellectual tools of critical thinking necessary to evaluate information free from the preconceptions of others.**

Critical thinking is a skill that is developed throughout life. Learning to improve thinking, like learning other skills, takes practice. Just as initial attempts to ride a bike may be clumsy, you may feel awkward as you undertake the structured approach to critical thinking described in this book. This book builds on your current critical thinking skills. As you become more proficient, you will become more comfortable and willing to increase the complexity of the communications you analyze. In a changing environment it is important to be able to sort through information found in a variety of sources to make decisions about what to believe. This book is designed to help you defend yourself against weak evidence and misleading reasoning.

Evaluating Psychological Information is intended to be used with your introductory psychology textbook. Study this book after reading your textbook chapter on how psychologists do research. Use your textbook for the definitions of the terms related to psychological research used in this book.

After you have previewed the chapters, start with Chapter 1 and work straight through the book. Skipping around is likely to increase your study time. Completion of the activities in *Evaluating Psychological Information* will sharpen your critical thinking skills and enable you to apply these skills to psychological material you read, see, or hear in the mass media. In addition, you can use critical thinking skills to evaluate your own statements and presentations of evidence to improve your persuasive communication.

The examples and exercises in this book were created for demonstration and may not accurately reflect the results of psychological research.

Chapter 1
Introduction to Critical Thinking

Tips for Studying Each Chapter
1. Read the *"Preview"* to obtain an overview of the chapter.
2. Read the *"Key Questions"* which indicate what you are to learn from the chapter.
3. Read the chapter to answer the *"Key Questions."*
4. Answer the questions in *"Check Your Understanding"* and *"Practice"* to provide review for the important ideas and skills, and then check your answers.
5. Answer the questions in the *"Exercises"* to sharpen your critical thinking.
6. Answers are provided in the *"Appendix"* for the first *"Exercise"* in each chapter.

Preview Critical thinking is one of the most important skills you will sharpen in college. This chapter is an introduction to thinking critically about psychological information.

Key Questions To Guide Your Learning
☐ When is critical thinking used?
☐ Why is sharpening critical thinking skills important?
☐ How do primary and secondary sources differ?
☐ What will you learn from this book?

■ When Is Critical Thinking Used?

Psychological information comes at us from every direction. The morning newspaper describes a "cure" for depression. A radio interview features the effects of TV on children. An evening television program reports on a new way to help handicapped citizens. A magazine explores the issue of the impact of preschool education on intelligence. Students in one class might hear research on the limitations of eyewitnesses. Students in another class might view a film on the chemistry of drug addiction. An article on the Internet claims that a woman can identify colors through her fingertips. Everyday conversations are sprinkled with talk about the need to improve the thinking of students, the effects of physical punishment on children, and ideas on how to develop your powers of persuasion. Out of this mass of information, how do you know what to believe?

How accurate and dependable is the information we receive? All of us use this information to understand others and ourselves. We make decisions based on this information. Unfortunately, much of the psychological information we encounter is incorrect, incomplete, or misleading. If inaccurate information is believed, it could easily lead to poor decisions. How do we decide which information to believe?

Critical thinking is deciding what to believe and how to use information after a careful evaluation of the evidence and reasoning in a communication.

These processes are not new to you. You already question and judge information when making purchases. You raise questions and evaluate the quality of products and what salespeople tell you. This book is designed to help you sharpen your critical thinking skills as you encounter psychological information. Besides evaluating psychological information, you can use your critical thinking skills to evaluate information on education, medical treatments, and the social sciences. In addition, you may use critical thinking when deciding which college courses to take, which apartment to rent, which job will best meet your needs, which ads to believe, and which candidates to vote for. The boxes below are designed to further your understanding of critical thinking.

Terms Similar to Critical Thinking	Terms Dissimilar to Critical Thinking
analyze, appraise, assess, critique, evaluate, examine, grade, inspect, investigate, judge, measure, observe, rate, research, scrutinize, study, survey, weigh	biased, confused, deceived, distorted, fake, false, faulty, flawed, imprecise, inaccurate, incredible, incorrect, mislead, mistaken, mixed up, nonsense

A four step procedure to sharpen your critical thinking will be examined in the following chapters.

Step 1: Identify the source.
Step 2: Read to understand.
Step 3: Identify the research evidence.
Step 4: Evaluate the research evidence.

Critical thinking does not mean focusing on negative criticism or being overly critical on unimportant issues. Critical thinking includes raising and answering questions about information and is useful when faced with deciding what to believe. Critical thinking is one of the most important thinking skills you will develop in college. After college, critical thinking is heavily used in certain types of jobs, such as: consultants, critics (art, book, music and film), doctors, editors, experts, inspectors, judges, lawyers, nurses, professors, psychologists, reporters, researchers, teachers, and jurors.

■ Why Is Sharpening Critical Thinking Skills Important?

The number of magazine and newspaper articles dealing with psychological topics has dramatically increased in recent years. Also, the Internet has made available large amounts of psychological information. Let's look at five examples from the mass media in which information was incorrect, incomplete, or misleading.

- Every year at Halloween, I read one or two newspaper articles about the danger of Halloween sadists - people who try to harm children as they move about our neighborhoods collecting candy. It seems to be common knowledge that these people have done great damage over the years. Some hospitals will x-ray candy to be sure it is safe. In 1985 Joel Best set out to discover how many children had been hurt at Halloween. He checked over a 20 year period in four different newspapers, in magazine indexes, and in the medical literature. He found: "In sum, although incidents of Halloween sadism do occur, we found no evidence that any child has been killed or seriously hurt by an anonymous Halloween sadist" (The myth of the Halloween sadist, *Psychology Today*, pp. 14-16). Best said that most cases of tampered candy were due to the "victim" who was probably playing a prank and/or looking for attention.

- Advertising in this country has come under attack for being misleading. Consider the statement: "Government tests have proven that no pain reliever is stronger or more effective than our aspirin." Is it reasonable to infer that this aspirin is the strongest and most effective pain reliever? Actually, those same government tests showed that the other pain relievers were equally effective.

- In 1988, John Cannell, a West Virginia medical doctor, contacted the education departments of 50 states and discovered that all reported their students' overall performance to be above average. At the same time, several national assessments had reported how poorly United States students were doing in comparison with students of other countries.

- Besides receiving incorrect and incomplete information, the American public is often misled. In 1994, Cynthia Crossen, a *Wall Street Journal* reporter, wrote a fascinating book entitled *Tainted Truth: The Manipulation of Fact in America*. She provided many examples of the twisting of facts dealing with advertising, opinion surveys, and supposedly "objective" research studies.

- Crime reporting by the mass media suggests we are experiencing a large increase in violent crime. *The Washington Post* on January 11, 1998, reported: "Since 1993, the homicide rate nationwide has dropped by 20 percent. Yet in the same period, the coverage of murders on the ABC, CBS, and NBC evening news has increased by 721%, according to the Center for Media and Public Affairs" (Schiraldi, 1998, January 11, p. C5).

It would be helpful if the information we received was accurate and thorough, rather than inaccurate, misleading, and incomplete. However, since psychology is such an interesting subject, the mass media often reports psychological news without the necessary information to allow us to decide what to believe.

■ How Do Primary and Secondary Sources Differ?

Having read several examples of incorrect, incomplete, and misleading information, consider the sources of psychological information you are likely to encounter in the future, such as newspapers, magazines, books and Internet information. Unless you become a psychologist, you will gain your psychological information from secondary sources rather than from primary sources.

What is a primary source? A source is considered primary when the person who reports the observations has personally experienced an event or conducted the research. Primary sources reporting original psychological research are usually found in technical journals and books. For example, the *Journal of Abnormal Psychology* and the *Journal of Educational Psychology* contain primary research reports.

What is a secondary source? A secondary source does not report original work but refers to the original work, observations, research, and opinions of others. Secondary sources, such as television, newspapers, radio, popular magazines, popular books, textbooks, and lectures, typically report in condensed form what others have said and done. A useful secondary source will accurately summarize a primary source without distortion. However, some secondary sources provide an incomplete and misleading picture of the process of collecting information and reporting research results.

Because most readers of psychological information use only secondary sources, this book will concentrate on developing the ability to think critically about secondary sources. Learning how to think critically about primary sources often occurs in upper-level psychology courses.

■ What Will You Learn From This Book?

Critical thinking is a process with three essential components: knowledge of a topic, a set of skills that can be used to evaluate both information and reasoning, and the attitudes to apply the knowledge and skills in deciding what to believe.

Knowledge The ability to identify and evaluate research evidence involves understanding differences between nonscientific and scientific evidence, the strengths and weaknesses of various types of psychological research, and the basic knowledge about the topic presented.

The basic knowledge about various psychological topics is presented in general psychology textbooks. The textbook chapter on psychological research provides a foundation for developing critical thinking skills. For example, you need to understand psychological terms such as random sampling, controlled variables, experimental and control groups, and cause and effect relationships.

Skills Thinking skills, such as understanding the viewpoint and arguments in a communication, analyzing the definitions of key terms, analyzing and evaluating the evidence, and evaluating the reasoning, are a second part of critical thinking. These thinking skills involve careful evaluation of the evidence and reasoning to decide what to believe.

Attitudes The third part of critical thinking involves wanting to use your thinking skills in appropriate situations. When psychological information is presented by others or by the mass media, do you suspend judgment until you have had a chance to think about what was presented? Do you spend time thinking to understand what was said? Do you search for reasons and evidence? Do you ask questions and evaluate what you have read or heard? Do you keep in mind that in psychology there are often several ways of looking at issues?

A knowledge of the facts and theories of psychology, along with an understanding of the way psychologists gather their facts, can influence your decisions. You will gain this knowledge from your psychology textbook and instructor. By studying the ideas in this book and working through the exercises, you will improve your critical thinking skills.

The goals for this book are

1. **To introduce you to a four step procedure to think critically both in the classroom and everyday life.**
2. **To improve your ability to think critically by evaluating research evidence and reasoning in secondary sources.**
3. **To increase your desire to think critically about psychological information.**

Chapter 1 has provided you with an overview of critical thinking. Chapter 2 discusses how to identify psychological research evidence. Chapters 3 and 4 describe a four step procedure to use in thinking critically about psychological information. Once you understand how to identify and evaluate psychological evidence you can become a more informed consumer of psychological information and be in a position to make better decisions.

Sharpening critical thinking skills involves practice and feedback. Few of us can learn to drive a car just by reading. All of us need practice and feedback to become proficient drivers. Consequently, completing the exercises in the spaces provided in this book is essential for learning. In addition, extensive feedback on your thinking is provided to guide your learning.

✓ Check Your Understanding for Chapter 1

Students learn from being active by writing answers in their own words. Develop your own chapter summary by answering these questions.

1.   **When is thinking critically used? (Include the four steps in your answer.)**

2.   **Why is sharpening your critical thinking skills important?**

3.   **How do primary and secondary sources differ?**

4.   **Identify the three secondary sources by placing an X next to each.**

    a.   ___ A research report where the researcher describes her observation.
    b.   ___ A textbook description of an experiment.
    c.   ___ A schizophrenic describing how he sees the world.
    d.   ___ A patient explaining what happened when she was in reality therapy.
    e.   ___ An artist describing why he had asked the model to come up to his studio.
    f.   ___ A researcher describing what he saw in a mental hospital.
    g.   ___ A newspaper summary of a research article on brain research.
    h.   ___ A researcher describing what others say they saw while visiting mental hospitals.

5.   **"Becoming an effective critical thinker involves knowledge, skills, and attitudes." Explain.**

If you have not read the "*Preface*," do so now. Then check your answers by using the "*Answer Key*" on the next page.

Answer Key
Check Your Understanding for Chapter 1

1. **When is thinking critically used? (Include the four steps.)**

   Critical thinking is used to decide what to believe. Critical thinking involves questioning, evaluating, and judging both evidence and reasoning in order to decide what to believe and what to do. A four step procedure will be explained in this book:

   Step 1: Identify the source
   Step 2: Read to understand
   Step 3: Identify the research evidence
   Step 4: Evaluate the research evidence

2. **Why is sharpening your critical thinking skills important?**

   Information presented in the mass media is often incorrect, incomplete, and misleading. Consequently, to be able to decide what information to believe, we need to critically think about that information.

3. **How do primary and secondary sources differ?**

   A primary source is the report of the observations of the writer. A secondary source reports the observations of others. Secondary sources usually condense what was in a primary source.

4. **Identify the three secondary sources.**

   b., g., h.   Each of these situations involves someone reporting information he or she did not observe directly.

5. **"Becoming an effective critical thinker involves knowledge, skills, and attitudes." Explain.**

   Critical thinking occurs when students understand how psychologists do research, have learned how to evaluate psychological evidence, and have the attitude that it is important to use their knowledge and skills to decide what to believe.

⊷ 1.1: Exercise in Careful Reading

"The Examination" An exercise in reading carefully.

Instructions Read the following story carefully. Then indicate whether you think the observations are correct, incorrect or questionable on the basis of the information presented in the story. Circle "C" if the observation is correct, circle "I" if the observation is incorrect, and circle "?" if the observation may be either correct or incorrect.

> A well-liked college psychology teacher finished assembling the final examination, placed it in a drawer, turned off all three lights in the office and went into the hall. Just then, a tall, dark figure appeared in the hall and demanded the examination. The teacher walked back into the office, turned on the three lights, and opened a drawer. Everything in the drawer was picked up and the tall individual ran down the hall. The head of the psychology department was called immediately.

Observations About the Story

1.	The thief was tall and dark.	C	I	?
2.	The teacher turned off the office lights.	C	I	?
3.	A tall figure demanded the examination.	C	I	?
4.	The examination was picked up by someone.	C	I	?
5.	The examination was picked up by the teacher.	C	I	?
6.	A tall, dark figure appeared after the teacher turned off the office lights.	C	I	?
7.	The man who opened the drawer was the teacher.	C	I	?
8.	The drawer contained the final examination.	C	I	?
9.	No drawer was actually opened.	C	I	?
10.	The head of the psychology department immediately learned about the missing examination.	C	I	?

Check your answers on p. 65 for Exercise 1.1 before doing Exercise 1.2.

☜ 1.2: Exercise in Careful Reading

"Arriving Home After Work" An exercise in reading carefully.

Instructions Read the following story carefully. Then indicate whether you think the observations are correct, incorrect or questionable on the basis of the information presented in the story. Circle "**C**" if the observation is correct, circle "**I**" if the observation is incorrect, and circle "**?**" if the observation may be either correct or incorrect.

> After riding home from work, you arrive late and notice that several lights are on in the study of your new home. You do not see anyone. Only one car is parked in front of your two story home, and "Bill Barclay, M.D." is printed in black letters on the driver's door. As you walk up to your home, you see that the car is empty. You walk into your home through the unlocked front door and go into the study.

Observations About the Story

1.	More than one light is on in your study.	C	I	?
2.	No car is parked in front of your home.	C	I	?
3.	There is only one car parked at your home when you arrive.	C	I	?
4.	The car parked in front of your home has lettering on at least one of its doors.	C	I	?
5.	You are getting home later than usual.	C	I	?
6.	Dr. Barclay drove the car to your home.	C	I	?
7.	The car parked in front of your home belongs to a man named Johnson.	C	I	?
8.	No one is at your home when you arrive.	C	I	?
9.	Your recently built home is two stories.	C	I	?
10.	There are exactly 12 black letters on the driver's door.	C	I	?
11.	After parking your car, you walk up to your home.	C	I	?
12.	The following events were in the story: you arrive home, you see a car, you walk up and into your home.	C	I	?

Chapter 2
Identify Psychological Research

Preview Psychologists conduct research to answer questions. When this research is described in secondary sources, you will need to identify the psychological research. There are three skills needed to identify the research. This chapter will assist you in developing these skills and review the key terms used in experimental research. Examples of psychological research will be reviewed.

Key Questions To Guide Your Learning
- How do you identify psychological research?
- What is a citation?
- What is included in the description of the study?
- What are the research results?
- What are the key terms of experimental research?

■ How Do You Identify Psychological Research?

Upon completion of their research, psychologists describe the way their study was done and the results. This information is published in journals and books. These reports are called primary research reports because the person who made the observations reports their observations. Upon occasion, you might read a primary research report. However, most of the time you will read a summary of that research described by someone other than the researcher. You will be getting information from secondary sources.

How do you identify psychological research found in secondary sources? Psychological research is based on careful observations. These careful observations are reported so that the reader can understand what was observed. To identify psychological research, look for three parts: (1) a citation, (2) a description of the study, and (3) the research results.

■ What Is A Citation?

The citation alerts the reader that there is a primary source which refers the reader to the primary research report where full details of the study are given. The citation is given just before or after the research is described and includes the last names of the researchers and the year the research report was published. At the end of the source you are reading, there will be references so you can find the original study. Most newspaper and magazine articles do not provide references.

When describing research, psychologists use phrases like these: "Jones (1981) observed . . . ," "Nelson (1983) conducted a study . . . ," "The evidence (Van, 1984) supported the hypotheses . . . ," "Able (1985) found . . . ."

■ What Is Included in the Description of the Study?

The description of the study provides information about the subjects and the procedure.

Subjects (or Sample) The subjects or sample are observed by the researcher. Who were the subjects? Were they humans or nonhumans? What were their characteristics? How were they chosen? How many were observed? Writers should indicate clearly who the subjects were and how they were selected.

Procedure The procedure states what was done to the subjects, the situation in which the subjects were placed, and the specific behaviors observed.

■ What Are the Research Results?

The research results state what was discovered from the observations of the subjects. Unfortunately, some writers include their personal views, which may not be based on careful observations. Consequently, a citation and result do not guarantee that the evidence is reliable. For important topics you may want to check the primary source.

A Good Example of psychological research in a secondary source.

> ". . . Latane and Rodin (1969) conducted an experiment built around a 'lady in distress.' In this experiment, a female experimenter asked college students to fill out a questionnaire. The experimenter then retired to the next room . . . A few minutes later, she staged an accident. What the students actually heard was the sound (from a hidden tape recording) of the young woman climbing a chair, followed by a loud scream and a crash, as if the chair had collapsed and she had fallen to the floor. Then they heard moaning and crying . . . Of those who were alone, 70 percent offered to help the young woman; of those who were participating in pairs with strangers, only 20 percent offered help." (This quote is from E. Aronson's book *The Social Animal,* 1988, p. 47. Go to the "References" at the end of this book to see a list of references.)

Here are the three parts of psychological research based on the above quote.

Citation to a Primary Source Latane and Rodin (1969). To check the full reference information you would need to check the list of references at the end of the book. Here is what was in the list of references: Latane, B., & Rodin, J. (1969). A lady in distress. *Journal of Experimental Social Psychology, Volume 5*, 189-202.

Description of the Study
Subjects - college students
Procedure - sentences two through seven

Research Results The research results are found in the last three sentences of the paragraph.

```
┌─────────────────────────────────────────────────────────────────────┐
│          Identify Psychological Research in Secondary Sources         │
│                                                                       │
│   1.  Citation                                                        │
│       Includes the researcher's last name and the year the research   │
│       (the study) was published, refers the reader to a primary       │
│       source in the list of references                                │
│                                                                       │
│   2.  Description of the study                                        │
│       a.  Sample - who was studied (the subjects)                     │
│       b.  Procedure - how the study was done                          │
│                                                                       │
│   3.  Results                                                         │
│       Based on observations of behavior                               │
│                                                                       │
└─────────────────────────────────────────────────────────────────────┘
```

■ What Are the Key Terms of Experimental Research?

In your psychology course you have studied experimental research. This section reviews the key terms of experimental research which are important to understand to be able to think critically about research. You may want to review your course materials on experiments and random sampling. Here is an analysis of the lady in distress experiment by Latane and Rodin (1969) described above.

Hypothesis A hypothesis is the best guess (a prediction) as to what condition or event might cause a change in behavior. Careful, controlled, repeated, and objective observations are made to determine if the hypothesis is supported or rejected. Psychological evidence in psychology doesn't **prove** a hypothesis. There is no hypothesis given in the quote from Aronson's *The Social Animal*.

Subjects The subjects are college students. No information is given about the number of subjects or about how the subjects were chosen. **Random sampling** is used to avoid biased results (incorrect results). Random selection means that each subject had an equal chance to be selected from the population (all those the researcher wishes to discuss). Psychologists are interested in knowing that their subjects are typical of the population. If the observed group is not representative (or typical) of the population, conclusions from the sample may not apply to the population. A representative sample (a random sample) is obtained through the process of random sampling.

Controlled Variables All subjects were asked to fill out a questionnaire, the experimenter left the room, and all subjects heard the woman experimenter in the next room scream, crash, and moan. The emergency was taped so that all the students heard the exact same sequence of events in the same way. The use of controlled variables is important to specify causes.

Independent Variable The independent variable was the size of the group who heard the emergency, either one person or a pair. All of the subjects in the alone condition were told exactly the same thing and heard the same emergency. All of the subjects in the pair condition were told exactly the same thing and heard the same emergency. The only difference between the two conditions was the number of persons present, either one or two, when the emergency happened.

Dependent Variable The dependent variable was the offering of help to the female experimenter. All subjects were observed to see if they would offer help to the lady in distress. The exact type of help that was offered was not explained.

Experimental and Control Groups In the experimental group the subject knew there was one other person listening to the crash and the call for help. In the control group the subject knew she alone was hearing the crash and the call for help.

Description of the Study The description of the study involved subjects being asked to fill out a questionnaire. While they were filling out the questionnaire, they heard the female experimenter climb onto a chair, fall from the chair, scream, moan, and cry.

Results The results were given in percentages: Seventy percent of the subjects who were alone offered to help the young woman who had just fallen; twenty percent of the subjects who were in pairs offered help.

Limited Circumstances Each research study takes place under specific and limited circumstances: the subjects are observed at a particular time and place with a specific procedure. Limited circumstances remind us that the observations were made under one set of circumstances and that the results may not apply in different circumstances. Limited circumstances are part of all research, not just experiments.

The limited circumstances here involved a study in a laboratory. The college students had a woman experimenter who fell and needed help in the room next door. The students could hear but not see the accident. The students were tested alone or with one other stranger. The subjects did not know the experimenter.

Now that the key terms of experimental research have been reviewed, check your understanding on the next page.

The Major Types of Psychological Research Evidence	
Descriptive Evidence	**Experimental Evidence**
Clinical Observations	Hypothesis
Correlational Studies	Independent Variable
Naturalistic Observations	Dependent Variable
Surveys	Controlled Variables
Tests	Experimental Group
	Control Group
(Check your textbook for	Random Assignment
explanations.)	Limited Circumstances

✓ Check Your Understanding for Chapter 2

Write answers in your own words.

1.   **What three things do you check for to identify psychological research in a secondary source?**

   a.   b.   c.

2.   **What is a citation? What is included in a citation?**

3.   **What two things are discussed in the description of a study?**

4.   **What are the research results?**

5.   **Explain how population, sample, and random sampling fit together. Describe an example of random sampling. (See your psychology textbook, if you need to review.)**

6.   **My friend John said: "I saw a group of people helping a woman move her stalled car. That proves that the more people present, the more help you get." Describe your thinking about this statement.**

Answer Key
Check Your Understanding for Chapter 2

1. **What three things do you check for to be able to identify psychological research evidence in a secondary source?**

    a. A citation.   b. The description of the study.   c. The research results.

2. **What is a citation? What is included in a citation?**

    A citation refers you to a reference at the end of the source. The reference listed at the end of the source could be located and would provide the full details of the research study. The citation must include the name of the researcher who reported the evidence and the year the report was published. Generally, the citation comes before the description of the study and the research results. See p. 11.

3. **What is discussed in the description of the study?**

    The description of the study involves providing information about the subjects and the procedure. Information about the subjects would include who the subjects are, their characteristics, their number, and how they were chosen. The procedure describes how the research was conducted and what was observed. See p. 12.

4. **What are the research results?**

    The research results indicate what was observed and what was discovered from doing the research. See p. 12.

5. **Explain how population, sample, and random sampling fit together. Describe an example of random sampling.**

    Psychologists are interested in large groups of people, but ordinarily observe just a small part of the group. The large group is called the population while the smaller group actually observed is called the sample or subjects. To make accurate statements about the population, the process of random sampling is used. In random sampling each member of the population has an equal chance to be chosen to represent the population. Random sampling is used to avoid bias.

    I want to know how many hours my General Psychology classmates studied for the final exam. My class of 200 students is the population and the sample is 10% or 20 students. I wrote down all 200 names on identical slips of paper, put them into a hat, and drew out 20 for my random sample. See p. 13.

6. **My friend John said: "I saw a group of people helping a women move her stalled car. That proves that the more people present, the more help you get." Describe your thinking.**

John is reporting his personal experience, not a research study. Even if I assume he accurately made and reported his observations, his evidence does not prove the statement that the more people present the more help given. His nonscientific evidence provides some support for that statement but is based on only one observation. There may be many unusual factors in the situation he observed. For example, all of the people might have previously been in the car and so were helping move their own car.

✓ Practice on Experimental Research Terms

For questions 1 through 9, place the letter of the correct answer on the line to the left. Then write your answer for question 10.

Questions 1 and 2 refer to the following paragraph.

☞ Fifty preschool children are randomly assigned to two groups by the flip of a coin. One group watches "Sesame Street" on TV every day for a week. The other group watches cartoons every day for a week. Both groups are then given a test that measures creativity in children.

____ 1. In this study, the independent variable is
    a. what the children watched on TV.
    b. how each child scored on the creativity test.
    c. the fifty preschool children.
    d. the test of creativity.

____ 2. In this experiment, the dependent variable is the
    a. children.
    b. content of the TV show.
    c. children's scores on the creativity test.
    d. children's ages.

Questions 3 to 6 refer to the following paragraph:

☞ An experiment was performed to test whether caffeine in Classic Coke would improve performance of freshmen college students on an intelligence test. One randomly chosen group of subjects was given an eight-ounce cup of Classic Coke containing caffeine to drink ten minutes before taking the intelligence test. Another randomly chosen group was given an eight-ounce cup of decaffeinated Classic Coke to drink ten minutes before taking the test. Neither group had any other food or drink for three hours before the experiment began.

___ 3. Why was one group given a cup of decaffeinated Classic Coke rather than being given nothing at all?
   a. so the subjects would have exactly the same experience except for the stimulant effect of caffeine
   b. so the subjects wouldn't get too hungry during the experiment
   c. so the subjects would be more cooperative in the experiment
   d. to make sure subjects were randomly chosen

___ 4. What is the independent variable in the experiment?
   a. not eating for three hours before the experiment
   b. the intelligence test score
   c. the amount of caffeine
   d. the taste of the beverage

___ 5. What is the dependent variable in the experiment?
   a. not eating or drinking for three hours before the experiment
   b. the intelligence test score
   c. caffeine
   d. decaffeinated Classic Coke

___ 6. Why were subjects prevented from eating or drinking for three hours before the experiment?
   a. to equalize the subjects' beliefs about what would happen
   b. to make the experiment like real life
   c. to control a factor that could affect the dependent variable
   d. to control the independent variable

___ 7. A reporter on a school newspaper wanted to know how the 5,000 students on her campus felt about some of the school's rules. Which approach is closest to obtaining a random sample?
   a. Interview the several dozen associates, friends, and classmates with whom she comes into contact each day.
   b. Interview as many students as she can as they come out of the student union.
   c. Pass out questionnaires to be filled in and collect them from students in the cafeteria during lunch.
   d. Send a questionnaire together with a stamped, self-addressed envelope to every 100th student on the student roster.
   e. Place a questionnaire in the school newspaper asking that it be completed and returned to the school newspaper office.

8. Which of the following examples is closest to being an unbiased sample (a random sample)?
   a. An opinion poll, checking on campus views, studied a sample that consisted of every tenth person who entered the student cafeteria.
   b. In a market survey of a new product for men and purchased by men, interviewers call during the day at every hundredth home.
   c. In order to assess consumer response to the latest farm price-support program, every tenth person randomly selected from a list of all the people in New York and Boston is contacted.
   d. A psychology professor wished to know if the 200 students in his course wanted a multiple-choice or essay exam. He drew 20 names from a hat containing the names of all the students.

9. Children imitate the violence they see in films. Which one of the following procedures best tests this hypothesis?
   a. A group of children is measured for aggression in a play situation. The most aggressive children are then shown one hour of a violent film. They are next observed on the playground to see if they are more aggressive than before the film.
   b. A group of children watches one hour of a violent film during a school day. Another group goes through a normal school day. At the end of the day, both groups are given a free play situation where observations of aggression are made.
   c. A group of children watches one hour of a violent film where an adult repeatedly hits a doll. Another group watches one hour of a film where an adult plays with a doll. Later in the school day both groups of children are given a doll to play with and observed. Subjects are tested individually.
   d. A group of children is observed at home after they watch one hour of a violent movie to see how often they hit a doll during 30 minutes of play.

10. Review the strengths and weaknesses of the psychological research methods listed in your textbook. On a separate sheet of paper jot down each method listed in your textbook and state the strengths and limitations of each approach.

   Example
   a. Naturalistic Observation - limitations
      1) It is difficult to specify causes.
      2) Waiting for events to occur takes time.
      3) Paying attention to all and only the important data is difficult.

Answers to Practice on Experimental Research Terms
Don't look at the answers until you have answered the questions yourself. Getting the answers is important, but it is more important to develop your thinking processes.

   1. a   2. c   3. a   4. c   5. b   6. c   7. d   8. d   9. c.

✓ Practice Finding the Psychological Research

Identify the citations and then identify the psychological research (citation, description, results). Assume that each citation has full reference information at the end of the article. The sentences are numbered for your convenience.

☞ (1) Should children be punished? (2) One view holds that children require physical punishment (Sock, 1986). (3) A recent survey done by Yale researchers found that 87 percent of parents do use physical punishment on their children. (4) Dr. Rough (1984), a child psychologist, wrote that it is better to spank a child who runs into the street than to just tell the child that cars are dangerous. (5) Johnson said in a letter to a local newspaper he had observed puppies hit on the nose (punished) who then stopped eating.

(6) Jones (1957, p. 423) defined punishment as "an unpleasant stimulus which occurs just after a response which decreases or stops the behavior." (7) In his novel *Walden Two* Skinner (1948), one of psychology's most eminent researchers, said that punishment is not effective. (8) Late (1950) did a study in which hungry white rats were trained to press a bar for food. (9) Half the rats were given shock and half were given no shock. (10) The rats given the shock decreased their bar pressing for a short time but returned to bar pressing as often as the unshocked rats.

(11) Solomen (1992) reported on a sample of high school seniors who scored in the top two percent on the SATs. (12) Ninety-five percent of them said that they had received punishment when they were children. (13) Eighty percent of a group of high school seniors who had scored in the bottom half of their graduating class reported they had been punished as children. (14) Canfield (1990) found that parents who physically punished their children had more aggressive children. (15) One hundred children, ages three and four, were rated by school teachers on their aggressiveness. (16) Mothers who had physically punished their children at least once in the previous month had children who were rated as aggressive. (17) The ten mothers who had not physically punished their children had children who were rated the least aggressive by the teachers.

1. List the other six citations. List the sentence number, author, and year.

	sentence	author	year
Example	(2)	Sock,	1986

_____

_____

_____

_____

_____

_____

2. List two more sentences that contain psychological research and the citation. Psychological research includes a citation, results, and the description of the study.

	sentence(s)	researcher(s)	year
Example	(8) - (10)	Late	1950

_____

_____

Do not go to the next page for feedback until you have completed this page.

Answers to Practice

1. List all of the citations. List the sentence, author, and year.

sentence(s)	author	year
(2)	Sock	1986
(4)	Rough	1984
(6)	Jones	1957
(7)	Skinner	1948
(8)	Late	1950
(11)	Solomen	1992
(14)	Canfield	1990

2. List the sentence(s) that contain the psychological research and the citation. Did you include all of the sentences for each research study?

sentence(s)	researcher(s)	year
(8) - (10)	Late	1950
(11) - (13)	Solomen	1992
(14) - (17)	Canfield	1990

Here is clarification of the citations that do not contain psychological research.

(2) Sock, 1986 - This sentence is an opinion.

(3) This sentence looks like research, but has no citation. Therefore, it is not research evidence.

(4) Rough, 1984 - This sentence is an opinion. There is no research evidence described here to support his opinion.

(5) Johnson - If there is no date, you do not have a citation.

(6) Jones, 1957 - This sentence is a definition.

(7) Skinner, 1948 - This sentence is an opinion without supporting research evidence.

In summary, to find psychological research

1. Look for the first author and a date (the year).
2. Decide if the information is psychological research.
3. If it is not psychological research, do you know what it is? (definition, hypothesis, theory, opinion, expert opinion, only a result)
4. Look for the next citation and date. Do steps 2 & 3 again until all citations are located and evaluated.

➥ 2.1: Exercise in Thinking Critically

Identify the citations and then identify the psychological research. Assume that each citation has full reference information at the end of the article.

☞ (1) Do you feel guilty after telling a lie? (2) What can you do to get rid of that feeling? (3) Festinger (1957) wrote a book entitled *A Theory of Cognitive Dissonance* which explains why people feel uneasy. (4) He called the uneasy feeling dissonance, and he said dissonance occurs whenever a person has two inconsistent beliefs. (5) Aronson (1968) explained that dissonance is often so uncomfortable that people try to reduce the dissonance. (6) For example, telling a lie is inconsistent with seeing ourselves as being honest and we experience dissonance. (7) Is there any evidence to support this theory? (8) Festinger and Carlsmith (1959) asked college students to do a boring task of turning pegs. (9) Then they persuaded each subject to tell the next student that the task was interesting, which was a lie. (10) Half the subjects received $20 to tell the lie and be available to play the same role the rest of the semester while the other half received $1. (11) After the lie had been told, all subjects were interviewed and asked to rate how interesting the peg turning task was. (12) Subjects who told a lie for $1 reduced their dissonance by convincing themselves that they had not told a lie. (13) They rated the task as more interesting than subjects paid $20. (14) Aronson and Carlsmith (1963) found that 11 children given a mild threat not to play with a toy decided that the toy was really not that special while 11 children given a severe threat actually increased their liking for the toy. (15) So far, this research has dealt with people's attitudes, not their behavior. (16) Is there research on behavior change? (17) Freedman (1965) found that a mild threat will reduce a child's actual playing with a very attractive, forbidden toy (a robot) more than a severe threat. (18) Three weeks after receiving the threats children were given the chance to play with toys and the robot. (19) Few children who had received the mild threat played with the robot while most of the severely threatened children played with the robot. (20) Soronson (1989) believes that dissonance theory can be used to teach children. (21) Psychological research supports Festinger's theory of cognitive dissonance.

1. List all of the citations. List the sentence, author, and year.

	sentence	author	year
Example	(3)	Festinger	1957

_____

_____

_____

_____

_____

2. List the sentences that contain psychological research, then the researcher(s), and year.

sentence(s)	researcher(s)	year

_____

_____

_____

Answers are on p. 65.

✍ 2.2: Exercise in Thinking Critically

Identify the citations and then identify the psychological research. Assume that each citation has full reference information at the end of the article. "The Bystander Effect" by Ed Jones (1995). *Journal of Social Psychology*, page 248.

☞ (1) Will people help less often in a crisis when there are bystanders present? (2) Latane and Darley (1968) had college subjects fill out a questionnaire in a room either alone or with two others. (3) The experimenters introduced smoke into the room and observed the subjects. (4) Seventy-five percent of the alone subjects reported the smoke, while only thirteen percent of the together subjects reported any smoke. (5) In a second study, Latane and Rodin (1969) had male college subjects hear a "lady in distress" in the next room. (6) She fell off a chair and screamed loudly for help. (7) Seventy percent of the alone subjects helped, while only 20 percent of the subjects who were in the presence of another helped. (8) Darley and Latane (1968) had subjects participate in a group discussion in which another subject appeared to have a seizure. (9) The subjects either thought they were in the discussion just with the seizure victim or thought that others were present in different rooms. (10) Eighty-five percent of the alone subjects helped while only thirty-one percent helped when the subject thought that others were also listening. (11) These three experiments support the view that the larger the group the fewer the bystanders who will intervene. (12) However, Piliavin, Rodin, and Piliavin (1969) found that 95 percent of the time help was given to a man who fell to the floor of a subway car when a number of bystanders were present. (13) Their data offered no support for the bystander hypothesis. (14) Long (1989) explained that the bystander hypothesis means that the presence of others decreases actual helping in a crisis. (15) Bills (1992) thought that an important difference in the studies is that in the subway study the bystanders could see that a person needed help whereas in the lady in distress study she was in another room where she could be heard but not seen.

1. List all of the citations by sentence.
    sentence(s)   author(s)   year

    _____
    _____
    _____
    _____
    _____
    _____

2. List the sentences for the psychological research, then the researcher(s), and year.
    sentence(s)   researcher(s)   year

    _____
    _____
    _____
    _____

Chapter 3
Thinking Critically About Secondary
Sources in Psychology:
The First Two Steps

Preview This chapter explains Steps 1 and 2 of a four step procedure for thinking critically about written sources; Steps 3 and 4 are discussed in Chapter 4. The explanation of each step starts with an overview and is followed by discussion, examples, and then practice. Write your answers in the space provided. Answers to the practice sections are given after each practice so that you will know immediately how you are doing.

Key Steps To Guide Your Learning
☐ Step 1: Identify the source.
☐ Step 2: Read to understand.

■ Step 1: Identify the Source

Identify who wrote the source, where it was published, and when.

Overview Identifying a source is important for two reasons: (1) If you learn something valuable from a source, you may wish to identify the source of that information in a conversation or written work. (2) As you continue reading on a topic, you will recognize certain authors. Authors who do not give evidence or who use poor reasoning are worth less of your time than authors who provide reliable evidence and logical reasoning.

Discussion Knowing the qualifications of the writer can be important. Readers tend to have higher confidence in writers who extensively study a topic, present evidence both for and against their view, use careful reasoning, and state conclusions based on the presented evidence.

Readers can place more confidence in observers who were present at the event, were skilled in making observations, used precise techniques, and had no preconceptions about the results.

In general, readers should expect higher accuracy from writers who are reporting their own observations (primary sources) than from writers summarizing the research of others (secondary sources). Writers of secondary sources must guard against taking material out of context. When readers decide what to believe, both types of sources must be carefully considered.

Knowing where the information was published can provide a clue about the quality of what will be read. Scientific publications evaluate the evidence that writers wish to publish and require that related information be presented. These publications have a reference page at the end of the article. Some publications pursue the big headline, tell only part of the story, are careless with evidence, and draw conclusions beyond their evidence. These publications seem to believe that their readers either have no critical thinking skills or will not take the time to think critically.

Although it is important to identify a source, knowing who wrote the article and where it was published are not always useful in evaluating a source. Why? Unfortunately, too many experts do not deliver dependable information. Consequently, pay more attention to evidence and reasoning than to credentials.

Be sure to note the publication date of the secondary source. The field of psychology is constantly changing and evidence that was an accurate description of reality in the past may not represent current reality. For example, during the 1940s, research suggested that women conformed more than men. Do women conform more than men today? Older findings may still be valid, but the writer should bring current research to the reader's attention. The following examples indicate how to cite secondary sources.

To Identify an Article Identify the authors last names, the name of the publication in which the article was published, and the year the article was published.

> **How would you identify this source?** When will people help in a crisis? by John M. Darley and Bibb Latane. Reprinted from *Psychology Today,* December 1968, Ziff-Davis Publishing Company.

> **Answer** Darley and Latane, *Psychology Today,* 1968. (The question "Where was it published?" does not imply a city or town. The place of publication is either a newspaper, magazine, journal, or book.)

To Identify a Book Identify the author's last name, the title of the book (capitalize the first word only), and the year the book was published.

> **How would you identify this source?** *Love Is Never Enough* by Aaron Beck, New York, Harper and Row, 1988.

> **Answer** Beck, *Love is never enough*, 1988.

✓ Practice in Step 1: Identify the Source

Identify these sources before checking your answers.

1. Able and Son, "Punishment," in *American Psychologist*, 1988, volume 7, p. 42.

   Write your answer here: _____

2. Johnson, Sara, *Intelligent Behavior*, Fellow Publishers, Chicago, 1995.

   Write your answer here: _____

Answers To Practice

1. Able and Son, *American Psychologist*, 1988.

2. Johnson, *Intelligent behavior*, 1995.

■ Step 2: Read to Understand

What is the author's central idea? What are the key points? What three words are often misused? What are five propaganda techniques?

Overview Step 2 involves understanding what is being said. Writers organize their message around a central idea and key points. How do you know when you understand an article? You understand an article when you are able to accurately summarize the article in your own words, detect the misuse of "proof," "random," and "average," and identify propaganda techniques.

Discussion To understand an article, find the central idea. A central idea is sometimes called the main idea, a thesis, a conclusion, a purpose, or the writer's opinion on a topic. The central idea is often stated near the beginning or the end of an article. Some writers don't precisely state the central idea but only supply hints. Therefore, you may need to read the article more than once to identify the central idea.

The central idea builds on the key points. The key points (sometimes called main points) should be related to the central idea. Deciding whether to believe each key point depends on the evidence used to support each key point. When reading psychological sources, it is important to determine what evidence is presented for each key point.

When reading to understand, note the words "prove (proves)," "random sample," and "average" which are often misused. Psychological research either supports or does not support the hypothesis. Psychological observations do not prove a hypothesis or signify proof. Rarely is the word "proves" or "proof" used correctly when dealing with psychological information.

"Random sampling" implies that all in the population had an equal chance of being studied and that the possibility of bias (mistaken evidence) is small. Some authors will label a sample as **random** but indicate that the selection method was one of picking subjects from those walking down the street. That process is not random. Random sampling means that all members of a population had an equal chance of being selected to be in the sample. Nonrandom sampling can easily lead to incorrect conclusions.

A third word often misused is "average." Average can signify "mean," "median," or "mode." The "mean" is the arithmetic average while the "median" is the middle-most score, and the "mode" is the score that occurs most often. Writers often speak of the average but don't define which average is being used. Review in your textbook if you need further information on mean, median, and mode.

Propaganda techniques are used to persuade through the use of emotion rather than through critical thinking. Listed below are five common propaganda techniques.

The Bandwagon The reader is asked to uncritically accept something since supposedly everyone else has.

> **Example** "Everyone agrees that college students are too concerned about making money."

Extreme Statements Some writers are not careful and use extreme statements when discussing evidence. The following words when applied to psychological topics are usually exaggerations or false: "all," "every," "completely," "entirely," "always," "none," "never," "no exceptions."

> **Example** "Positive reinforcement with children and adults is always more effective than punishment." How does the writer know that positive reinforcement is always more effective than punishment?

Glittering Generalities Appeals to emotions through using "good words" to draw attention away from the ideas and evidence.

> **Examples** "dramatic evidence," "conclusive," "the best," "the most important"

Namecalling Appeals to hate and fear by labeling the source with "bad names" to draw attention away from the evidence.

> **Examples** "manipulator," "crazy," "deceitful"

Testimonial The reader is asked to accept uncritically a position because someone important or popular believes the position.

> **Example** "Dr. Knower, a well-known psychologist, says that . . . ."

Step 1 of critical thinking involves identifying the source of information both in the classroom and in informal discussions. Knowing the source allows you to check your information, if necessary. Knowing the date lets you know if the source is current.

Step 2 involves understanding exactly what the author is saying. It is a good study habit to summarize what the author says in your own words. You retain information longer if you have thought about what you are learning by putting the author's central idea and key points into your own words. Persuasion sometimes occurs through the use of misused words and propaganda techniques. Being able to spot such attempts at persuasion allows you to decide if you wish to be persuaded.

✓ Practice in Step 2: Read to Understand

1. Read to understand.
   a. What is meant by the phrase "the central idea of an article"?

   b. What is meant by the phrase "key points"?

2. Indicate whether "random" is used correctly or incorrectly in each sentence. If it is used incorrectly, explain why it is not random.

   a. We wanted to get a random sample of all college students at our college, so last Friday we interviewed every fifth person coming out of the college library at 9 p.m.

   b. We took a random sample of the general psychology class by writing the names of all of the students in the class on equal size pieces of paper, putting them all into a hat, and then drawing out twenty percent of the names.

3. For each statement identify the propaganda technique.

   a. _____ Recent dramatic research indicated that children who attend a preschool completed high school at a higher rate than similar children who did not attend preschool.

   b. _____ Although psychologists think that punishment is not effective, every parent knows just how effective punishment can be when used correctly.

   c. _____ Research has shown that the unemployed would work if there were available jobs. This research was done by ivory tower sociologists who know little about these people.

   d. _____ B. F. Skinner, an important psychologist, says that punishment is not effective.

   e. _____ The evidence entirely supports the view that internal rewards are most powerful.

Answers To Practice

Do not review the answers until you have completed the practice. Thinking skills rarely improve unless practiced.

1. a. The central idea is the conclusion that the author tries to get readers to accept.

    b. The key points are conclusions related to the central idea which require evidence. The critical thinker reads to find the author's evidence.

2. a. "Random sample" is used incorrectly in the first item. Fewer students may attend class on Friday, and students leaving from one building are probably not a representative sample of all students, particularly at 9 p.m.

    b. "Random" is used correctly in the second statement. Each class member had an equal chance of being chosen.

3. Label the propaganda techniques.
    a. Glittering generality: The glittering word "dramatic" is used.

    b. Bandwagon: "Every parent knows." Does every parent know this? Probably not.

    c. Name calling: The phrase "ivory tower sociologists" is trying to persuade us to reject the research and ignore the evidence by labeling the researchers in a negative way.

    d. Testimonial: The reader is asked to accept the idea that punishment is not effective because B. F. Skinner said so.

    e. Extreme statement: Rarely does the evidence in psychology "entirely" support any hypothesis.

The First Two Steps to Thinking Critically

Step 1: Identify the Source
    a. Who wrote the source? Include all of the authors.
    b. Where was it published? Name the journal, book or newspaper.
    c. When was it published (year)? Is this a recent source?

Step 2: Read to Understand
    a. State in your own words the central idea.
    b. State the key points.
    c. Note instances of the misuse of these words: "proves," "random," "average."
    d. Label any propaganda techniques: bandwagon, extreme statements, glittering generalities, name calling, testimonials.

Name _____   Date _____

☞ 3.1: Exercise in Thinking Critically

1.   Read to understand. Write your answers on the lines provided.

☞   (1) Preschool education is valuable for children. (2) Preschool education is the education of children ages three through five in school settings with teachers who have earned at least a four-year college degree. (3) Research proves that children who do not go to preschool do not play well with their peers and later are less successful in school. (4) Highly significant research by Jones (1988) clearly demonstrates that average children who had attended preschool were more likely to graduate from high school and were less likely to receive a criminal conviction. (5) Piaget, the famous Swiss psychologist, agrees that preschool education is important. (6) In fact, some child psychologists in New York believe that preschool education improves creativity for all children.

a.   State the central idea in your own words followed by the sentence number.

_____

b.   List two words used incorrectly (proves, random, average). Explain the misuse.
sentence   word   explain the misuse

_____

_____

c.   Identify and label four propaganda techniques.
sentence   word(s)   label the propaganda technique

_____

_____

_____

_____

2.   Label the propaganda techniques in the following examples:

a.   _____ Some people say that spanking is harmful to children. If you would check with your neighbors, you would find that they had been spanked and use spanking with their children.

b.   _____ The eminent psychologist Freud said that dreams are meaningful.

c.   _____ Punishment is a complex subject; however, parents who want their children to grow up right, be intelligent, and be the best they can be should realize that children need sound discipline.

d.   _____ People who disagree with me do not know what they are talking about and are trying to unfairly manipulate my emotions.

e.   _____ You should always refrain from using physical punishment on children.

Answers are on p. 65.

☞ 3.2: Exercise in Thinking Critically

This brief article by Dr. Anna Sound is "TV: Turn It Off," *Parents Monthly Review*, June 13, 1997, page 17. Use your critical thinking skills to answer the questions that follow this article.

☞ (1) Ninety-nine percent of American homes have television and the average child watches over twenty-six hours each week. (2) Research has clearly established these facts. (3) Because of the harm done to children, parents should limit the television watching of their children.

(4) What do children see on television? (5) Aggression has become increasingly important in television programs (Gerbner, 1990). (6) In 1954 Gerbner's research found that seventeen percent of the prime time programs (8-11 p.m.) had aggression as a main theme. (7) By 1990, Gerbner found that eighty percent of prime time programs contained aggression while almost all cartoons included aggression. (8) Gerbner's research also has shown that every three minutes an aggressive act occurs on Saturday morning cartoons.

(9) What is the effect of watching aggression on television? (10) Watching aggression on TV always increases children's aggressive acts. (11) Wrestle (1996) found using fifty four-year-old boys that the more murders that a boy sees on television the more often he will hit other children during fifteen minute play periods. (12) Casway (1986) observed 158 fifth grade boys in a study at Yale University and found that the boys who watched more violent programs were found to be less cooperative, less successful in interpersonal relationships, and less happy than boys who watched less violent programs." (13) Everyone can see that this evidence proves the disastrous damage done by television.

(14) Pat (1987) videotaped and then analyzed all of the evening shows (7 to 11 p.m.) for ABC, CBS, and NBC. (15) She found that television does not give an accurate picture of society. (16) Pat also found that murder and assault occur most often on television, while in real life, burglary and larceny occur most often. (17) Lot (1984) studied a random sample of adult heavy viewers (those who watch more than four hours of television each day) and found that they see the world differently than adult light viewers (viewers who watch less than two hours of television daily). (18) The heavy viewers who were interviewed individually and asked to respond to ten statements about women tended to believe cultural stereotypes about women more than light viewers. (19) In addition, they overestimate the danger of violence to themselves in real life. (20) This research is proof that viewing television is destructive to all viewers.

Step 1:   Identify the source.

    a. Who wrote the source? _____

    b. Where was it published? (Title of the journal or book)

       _____

    c. When was it published?   _____

Step 2:   Read to understand.

    a.   State the central idea in your own words followed by the sentence number.

          _____

    b.   Describe the other key points. The first one is done for you.

	sentence	key point
Example	(1)	American children watch a lot of TV.

          _____
          _____
          _____

    c.   Which words are used incorrectly? List the sentence number and the word (proves, random, average). Explain the misuse.

	sentence	word	explain the misuse
Example	(1)	average	not clear which average is meant

          _____
          _____
          _____
          _____

    d.   Identify and label any propaganda techniques. List the sentence number, the word or words, and label the propaganda technique.

	sentence(s)	word(s)	label the propaganda technique
Example	(2)	clearly established	glittering generality

          _____
          _____
          _____
          _____

Step 3:   Identify the research evidence. Write the sentence number(s) and the citation.

	sentence(s)	author	year
Example	(5) - (8)	Gerbner	1980

          _____
          _____
          _____
          _____

Chapter 4
Identify and Evaluate the Research Evidence

Preview Steps 3 and 4 focus on first identifying psychological research in secondary sources. You will be shown how to evaluate that evidence by checking information about the subjects, the procedure, and the results.

Key Topics To Guide Your Learning
- □ Step 3: Identify the research evidence.
- □ Step 4: Evaluate the research evidence.

■ Step 3: Identify the Research Evidence

Look for the evidence presented by the writer. Can you identify the psychological research?

Overview After becoming clear on what an author is saying through careful reading (Step 2), how do you decide which statements to believe? Evidence is the information used to decide which statements to believe. In the field of logic, a statement is a sentence that can be judged as either true or false, proven or not proven. In psychology, evidence does not prove or disprove a statement. Rather, psychologists deal with statements judged as probably true or probably false based on evidence that comes from systematic and careful observations of behavior.

Time and effort would be saved if the psychological statements encountered in the mass media were accurate. However, neither having a Ph. D. in psychology nor holding the position of an editor for a major newspaper guarantees an accurate and complete presentation of the evidence. Consequently, as a careful reader you need to do your own evaluation of the evidence.

If you are reading for pleasure and do not plan to use the evidence in decision making, there is little reason for moving to Steps 3 and 4 for evaluating an article. When you wish to be entertained, skim your source and then move on to something else. Such reading is similar to escape reading. However, if you are reading to understand psychological information so that you can use it, then evaluating the evidence and reasoning becomes important.

Discussion When reading a secondary source, what type of evidence is presented? It is important to separate the scientific research evidence from the nonscientific evidence. Then separate the incomplete research evidence from the research evidence.

1. **How do you identify the psychological research evidence?** As mentioned previously, to locate psychological research look for the three parts: (1) a citation, (2) a description of the study, and (3) the research results.

Citation Writers of secondary sources do not produce the research they cite. Therefore, they need to give credit to those who did the research by citing within the article the researcher and the year of the primary research report and by giving full reference information on the references page at the end of the article. *Look for the citation.*

Research Results Psychological research produces results based on the observations made by the researcher. *Look for the research results.*

Description of the Study In order to evaluate the research evidence, information must be given about the subjects and how the observations were made. All psychological research evidence is based on observations made in certain limited circumstances. Even if only a brief description of the study is given, label that statement as research evidence. *Look for the description of the study.*

In review, identify psychological research evidence by looking for a citation, the research results, and at least some description of how the study was conducted.

2. **How do you identify incomplete research evidence?** Sometimes a research result is accompanied by a citation, but no description of the study is given. If you had access to the original study, you could learn how the evidence was obtained. Writers who give only the research results are asking you to accept that the research does in fact apply to the central idea presented by the writer and that it has been fairly and accurately represented. As a reader, you are not in a position to evaluate research evidence if there is no description of how the research was conducted. This evidence is considered incomplete and is called incomplete research evidence. Consequently, reserve judgment until you know more about how the research was done.

Research evidence in a secondary source requires a citation, results, and at least some description of the study. Some writers will cite several research studies and include their own research among the studies. When writers describe their own research, they may not refer the reader to the more detailed primary report. If these writers present only the results and do not state how the study was conducted, label these studies as incomplete research evidence.

A theory in psychology results when a psychologist pulls together several hypotheses and evidence. Usually, theories are well thought out and are supported by extensive research. When looking for psychological research, be alert for a statement of theory that is not supported by research evidence. In general, theoretical statements are broader than research results from one study. Theories, hypotheses, and psychological research all may have citations to indicate where the information came from. Only statements that include a description of the study based on observations are considered as research evidence.

When evaluating a source, look first for the scientific research evidence. However, for some topics you may be interested in weighing nonscientific evidence. Since the focus here is on scientific psychology, be alert for statements based on nonscientific evidence.

> ### Keys to Deciding What Is Research Evidence and What Is Incomplete Research Evidence
>
> 1. **Look for a citation (author and the year the study was published).**
>   If there is no citation (both the researcher and year are needed), you do not have research.
>
> 2. **Look for a research result.**
>   a. Does the result look like it is based on evidence obtained from careful and repeated observations of behavior?
>   b. If not, you do not have research evidence.
>
> 3. **Look for a description of the research.**
>   a. If there is a description of the study, label it as research evidence.
>   b. If there is no description of the study, label it as incomplete research evidence.

---

3. **How do you detect nonscientific evidence?** There are several types of nonscientific evidence. Readers do not expect evidence for opinions or value judgments. These statements are not based on carefully observed evidence. However, some authors use these statements as if they were reliable evidence.

Some writers use unsupported assertions. No citations or description of the study is provided. Phrases, such as "researchers have found," "psychologists believe," "psychologists hold," or "the research evidence demonstrates" do not count as citations. These general phrases do not indicate who did the research. Therefore, the reader cannot go to the primary report and review the description of how the evidence was gathered. Unsupported assertions have no evidence.

Readers will often come across other types of nonscientific evidence. Personal experiences and secondhand reports may be based on observations, but not systematic observations with careful controls. Such uncontrolled observations are often selective, biased, incomplete, and distorted.

> ### Types of Evidence Found In Secondary Psychological Sources
>
> | Nonscientific Evidence | Scientific Research Evidence |
> | --- | --- |
> | Opinions | Based on observations of |
> | Value judgments | behavior |
> | Unsupported assertions | Repeated |
> | Personal experiences | Objective |
> | Secondhand reports | Not biased |
> | | Controlled |
> | | Precise |

Here are some of the problems that occur when nonscientific evidence is used.

- ☐ An example (one observation) or the observations from only a few people may be used as evidence. It may not be clear who actually made the observations and under what conditions.

- ☐ The observations are not repeated and carefully checked.

- ☐ Observations are not written down as they occur but are recalled at some later date.

- ☐ The people being observed, usually those who are available, are rarely representative of a larger population.

- ☐ Important terms are not precisely defined and sometimes the definitions of key terms change throughout the article.

- ☐ A comparison group or comparison condition is rarely available.

- ☐ Control over important variables is impossible. It is very difficult to keep constant the relevant factors to be able to state a specific cause. Subtle factors can be overlooked.

- ☐ All of the evidence is not used. Evidence that is contrary to a statement is often overlooked, or only part of the evidence is selected.

- ☐ Some writers have biases which interfere with objective observation and make it difficult to separate evidence from opinions and value judgments.

In summary, the various types of nonscientific evidence were briefly mentioned to indicate that some statements in an article might not fall into the category of scientific research evidence. You do not need to be able to distinguish the various types of nonscientific evidence. However, when evaluating a source, identify the research evidence and the incomplete research evidence.

✓ Practice in Step 3: Identify the Research Evidence

These paragraphs were previously studied and are used here for further evaluation. Assume that all citations have full reference information given at the end of the book. This information is from Susan Rosenhouse, *An Introduction to Social Psychology*, 1997, p. 14.

☞ (1) Do you feel uneasy after telling a lie? (2) What do you do to get rid of that uneasy feeling? (3) Festinger (1957) put forth a theory of cognitive dissonance to explain why people feel uneasy. (4) He called the uneasy feeling dissonance, and said dissonance occurs whenever a person has two inconsistent beliefs. (5) The dissonance is often so uncomfortable that people try to reduce the dissonance. (6) For example, telling a lie is inconsistent with seeing ourselves as being honest and we experience dissonance. (7) Is there any research to support this theory? (8) Festinger and Carlsmith (1959) asked college students to do a boring task of turning pegs for about an hour. (9) Then they persuaded each subject to tell the next student that the task was interesting, which was a lie. (10) Half of the subjects received $20 to tell the lie and be available to help the rest of the semester while the other one-half received $1. (11) After the lie had been told all subjects were interviewed and asked to rate how interesting the peg turning task was. (12) Subjects who told a lie for $1 reduced their dissonance by convincing themselves that they had not told a lie. (13) They rated the task as more interesting than subjects paid $20. (14) Aronson and Carlsmith (1963) found that subjects given a mild threat not to play with an object decided that the object was really not that special, while subjects given a severe threat increased their liking for the object. (15) These studies have dealt with people's attitudes, not their behavior.

(16) Is there research on behavior change? (17) Freedman (1965) found that a mild threat ("I don't want you to play with the robot.") will reduce a child's actual playing with a very attractive, forbidden toy (a robot) more than a severe threat ("Do not play with the robot or I will take all the toys away."). (18) Three weeks after receiving the threats the children were given the chance to play with toys and the robot. (19) No child who had gotten the mild threat played with the robot while almost all of the severely threatened children played with the robot. (20) Psychological research supports Festinger's theory of cognitive dissonance.

Step 3: Identify the Research Evidence

Identify the research evidence and the incomplete research evidence. Research evidence (citation, description of the study, research results) often includes more than one sentence.

a.   Identify the incomplete research evidence.
    sentence(s)   researcher(s)   year

_____

b.   Identify the research evidence.
    sentence(s)   researcher(s)   year

_____
_____

Do not go to the next page until you have completed this page by writing your answers.

Answers to Practice for Step 3

a.   Incomplete research evidence
      (14) Aronson and Carlsmith, 1963. No specifics of the study are given. Mild **and severe** threat are not defined.

b.   Research evidence
      (8) - (13) Festinger and Carlsmith, 1959. Note the information that is given about **the study** and that all of the sentences relevant to the study are included in the psychological **research** evidence.
      (17) - (19) Freedman, 1965.

■ Step 4: Evaluate the Research Evidence

How good is the research evidence? What kinds of problems are there with **the research evidence?** Are there any problems with the reasoning relevant to the research evidence?

Overview To evaluate research evidence, it is important to know when the study was **published**, who the subjects were, how they were chosen, the way the study was done, and the results. **After** evaluating research evidence, evaluate the reasoning that ties the evidence to the key points. **Is the** evidence relevant to the key point? Does the evidence support the key point? Does the writer **draw** conclusions that go beyond the evidence?

Discussion Identify the research evidence in a source by citing the researcher and the **year of** publication. After summarizing the way the study was done (the description of the study) and **the** research results, decide if you have research evidence or incomplete research evidence. If you **have** incomplete research evidence, it is difficult to evaluate the study because so little information **is** given about the study. If you know how the research was done, use the questions below to **evaluate** the research evidence.

1.   **Citation** Who conducted the research and when? How recent is it? Current research **may** have modified older findings. Sometimes there is no recent research. However, the **writer** should indicate that information to the reader. Is any related research cited?

2.   **Subjects** Who are the subjects? What are their characteristics? How many are there? **How** were they chosen?

      Who are the subjects? If the writer is discussing humans, was the evidence **gathered** from humans? Evidence from animal research is just a hypothesis when applied to **humans** unless there is supporting research on humans or the writer convinces us that the **evidence** should apply to humans. If the results are applied to people, were both male and **female** subjects used? Were different age groups studied? What are the characteristics of **the** subjects?

      How many subjects were observed? Using observations from one or a few **subjects** is risky and likely to produce biased (not typical) results. Unusual and misleading **conclusions** can result from using small samples.

How were the subjects chosen? If a writer wishes to make comments about a group (the population) from studying only part of the group (a sample), it is essential that the selection procedure not be biased. Biased sampling can produce almost any evidence desired. Random sampling ensures that the sample will represent the population. Sometimes a writer will label a process as random, but you will discover that each subject did not have an equal chance to be chosen. If a random selection process was not used, was the process explained?

Sometimes writers **leave out** information about the subjects. Remember to ask these important questions:

- ☐ Who are the subjects?

- ☐ What are their characteristics?

- ☐ How many subjects were studied?

- ☐ How were they selected from the population? If a random process was used, was it explained?

Even if complete information is given about the subjects, there may be **problems** which decrease our confidence in the results. Ask these questions to determine possible problems dealing with the subjects.

- ☐ Are the subjects chosen relevant to the central idea and a key point? Has the writer overgeneralized the results from animals to humans? From college students to all people? From males to females?

- ☐ Were too few subjects studied to have confidence in the results? Experiments usually use the smallest number of subjects. Surveys need more subjects to generalize to populations.

- ☐ Was an unbiased sample studied? Was a random process used? If a random process was not used, who does the sample represent?

3. **Procedure** How was the study done? Are the psychological terms defined? How were the observations made? Even though you may label several sentences as research evidence, you may note that some important information is missing.

One difficulty in understanding psychological information is that many everyday terms have more precise or different meanings when used by psychologists. Other terms are not a part of everyday language. To understand a source, careful attention must be given to the definitions of the psychological terms.

Writers of psychological topics should define their terms so that the reader understands exactly what the writer is saying. If a writer does not define important terms, are the terms used consistently in the article? As you read more on psychological topics, you will become more familiar with important definitions so that you can evaluate a writer's use of a term from your own knowledge. If an unfamiliar term is used, use your textbook or a psychological dictionary to learn the meaning.

Writers on psychological topics should provide the reader with descriptions about how the independent variable and the dependent variable in the research were measured. Writers might discuss a topic referring to the construct definitions (broad definitions), but when citing research may not give operational definitions (specific definitions). Check to see that the independent and dependent variables have been precisely defined.

Constructs   Constructs are terms that refer to a variety of behaviors. "Aggression," "helping," "cognitive dissonance," "mental illness," "intelligence," and "learning" are all broad psychological terms called constructs. Psychologists use constructs to pull together related research for better understanding. Here is an example of a construct definition and its related operational definition:

> Construct definition -- Aggression is behavior intended to harm another.
> Operational definition -- Aggression is the behavior of person A (the subject) pushing a button to deliver an electric shock to person B whenever B gives a wrong answer.

Operational Definitions   Since constructs are broad terms, they cannot be studied directly. The construct must be redefined to state a specific aspect of behavior. Researchers must define exactly what they are going to observe and how they will measure behavior. If researchers do not use an operational definition, they might not be measuring the same behavior every time. Therefore, other researchers will not know exactly what behavior was observed.

The procedure of defining and measuring a specific part of a general term is called operationally defining the construct. Operational definitions are used in primary research reports and technical articles. Too often, operational definitions are missing from secondary sources, particularly for the independent and dependent variables.

Here are two examples of operational definitions:

> Conformity occurs when the subject states the incorrect answer after the group has stated an incorrect answer when asked the number of times a tone sounded.

> Learning is correctly answering 80 percent of the multiple choice questions on a ten-minute quiz (closed book) after studying the pages in the textbook on behavior modification.

Sometimes writers **leave out** important information about the procedure. Remember to ask these important questions:

- ☐ What factors have been controlled to produce reliable results?

- ☐ Was there a control group? If yes, how were subjects assigned to the experimental and control groups? Random assignment avoids bias.

- ☐ Is the independent variable precisely defined?

- ☐ Is the dependent variable precisely defined?

- ☐ What are the limited circumstances?

Even if complete information is given about the procedure, there may be **problems** which decrease our confidence in the results. Here are some of the possible problems dealing with the procedure.

- [] If there was no control group, then no cause and effect statement can be made. Misleading conclusions can easily occur when there is no comparison group.

- [] Was a reasonable control group used? Sometimes the control condition used is not the best one to use or there may need to be several control conditions.

- [] If subjects were not randomly assigned to the control condition, then the results might be due to differences in the groups rather than due to the independent variable.

- [] If other variables have not been controlled, these variables may produce the change in behavior rather than the independent variable.

- [] If subjects do not get the identical independent variable, that variability can influence the results.

- [] If the measurement of the dependent variable changes across subjects (if it is not reliable), the resulting variability can influence the results.

4. **Research Results** Are the results clearly and fully presented? How big is the difference among groups? Is it a statistically significant difference? If you need review on statistically significant, check your textbook.

Sometimes writers **leave out** information about the results. Remember to ask these important questions:

- [] Are specific results given?

- [] Are results given for each group studied?

- [] Is there an indication that the results were statistically significant?

If complete information is given about the results, there still may be **problems** which decrease our confidence in the results. Ask these questions to determine possible problems with the results.

- [] Are the results consistent with other research results on the topic?

- [] Are the results based on the reported research?

5. **Reasoning** How is the psychological evidence tied in with the central idea and key points? Does the evidence support the key points?

If you have no confidence in the research evidence, then the research evidence would not provide any support for the key points. Unless there is other relevant evidence, the key point would then be unsupported. Here are some problems dealing with reasoning.

- Is the research evidence relevant to the key points? Sometimes evidence is presented that is not directly relevant to the key point.

- Does the writer draw the correct conclusion from the evidence? Sometimes writers get careless and draw incorrect conclusions from the evidence.

- Does the writer generalize beyond the evidence? Some writers draw conclusions that go beyond the evidence. It is particularly important here to note who the subjects were and how they were selected.

- Was a control condition used for comparison? Conclusions based on research without a comparison condition need to be approached with caution.

- Was a cause and effect relationship based on research evidence other than an experiment? A correlation does not mean a cause has been isolated.

- A change in behavior is stated, but no measurements were made before the introduction of the independent variable.

- A survey was conducted but the sample was not randomly selected from the population. Conclusions cannot then be generalized to the population.

Evaluating Research Evidence In Secondary Sources

What is the research evidence for each key point?

1. **Citation** Who did the study and when? Is related research cited? Is recent evidence cited?

2. **Subjects** Who are the subjects? Their characteristics? Number? How selected? What is left out? What problems are there with the subjects?

3. **Procedure** How was the research done? Is there a control group? Were the subjects randomly assigned to groups? Are the independent and dependent variables precisely defined? Which other variables are controlled? What are the limited circumstances? What important information is left out? Are there any problems with the research?

4. **Results** What are the results? What is missing? Are there any problems with the results?

5. **Reasoning problems** Are there any reasoning problems? Does the evidence support the key points and central idea? Does the author draw conclusions that go beyond the evidence?

✓ An Example of Evaluating Research Evidence

Read this article which was previously studied and is used here for further evaluation. "The Bystander" by Ed Jones (1995). *Journal of Social Psychology*, page 248.

☞ (1) Will people provide help in a crisis? (2) Latane and Darley (1968) had sixty college freshmen fill out a questionnaire in a small room either alone or with two others. (3) The experimenters introduced white smoke into the room after ten minutes and observed the subjects. (4) Seventy-five percent of the alone subjects reported the smoke, while only thirteen percent of the together subjects reported the smoke.

(5) In a second study, Latane and Rodin (1969) had forty male college subjects hear a "lady in distress" in the next room. (6) The female experimenter went into the next room, fell off a chair, and screamed loudly for help (the accident was on tape). (7) Seventy percent of the alone subjects helped, while only twenty percent of the subjects who were in the presence of another helped.

(8) Darley and Latane (1968) had subjects participate in a group discussion in which another subject appeared to have a seizure. (9) The subjects either thought they were in the discussion just with the seizure victim or thought that others were present in different rooms. (10) Eighty-five percent of the alone subjects helped while only thirty-one percent helped when the subject thought that others were also listening. (11) These three laboratory experiments support the view that the larger the group the fewer the number of bystanders who will intervene. (12) However, Piliavin, Rodin and Piliavin (1969) found that ninety percent of the time help was given to a person who fell to the floor of a subway car when a number of bystanders were present. (13) Their data offered no support for the bystander hypothesis (the presence of others decreases helping behavior). (14) Apparently, bystanders don't help in the laboratory, but do help in real life.

Example How to evaluate the research evidence for sentences (2) to (4).

1. **Who did the study and when? Is related research cited? Is recent evidence cited?** Latane and Darley (1968) did the study described in sentences (2) - (4). Another 1968 study along with two 1969 studies are described. No recent research is cited.

2. **Who are the subjects? What are their characteristics? How many? How were they chosen? What is left out? What problems are there with the sample?** College freshmen were used. No further information is given about the characteristics of the sample. Sixty total subjects were studied. No information is given about how they were selected. It is not clear who these subjects represent.

3. **How was the study done? Is there a control group? Were the subjects randomly assigned to groups? Are the independent and dependent variables precisely defined? What other variables are controlled? What are the limited circumstances? What important information is left out? Are there any problems with the procedure?** Students were put into a room and asked to fill out a questionnaire. Some students were alone, while others were in the room with two others. The students were placed into two groups, an experimental group and a control group. The size of the group is the independent variable. Smoke was put into the room after 10 minutes, and the subjects were observed. Reporting the smoke was the dependent variable. The type of white smoke and amount were not explained. Did the smoke look and smell like fire? The

limited circumstances are that the study was done in a laboratory with some type of white smoke while subjects were filling out questionnaires.

4. **What are the research results? What is missing? Are there any problems with the results?** Seventy-five percent of those who were alone reported the smoke, while only thirteen percent of those who were with two others reported the smoke. To whom did the subjects report the smoke to? Only two size groups were studied.

5. **Are there any reasoning problems? How is the research evidence tied to the central idea? Does the author draw conclusions that go beyond the evidence?** The study doesn't state the type of smoke. Since the smoke was white, subjects together may have decided there was no emergency. Seventy-five percent versus thirteen percent seems to be a big difference. Why weren't bigger size groups used, such as five or ten subjects? The results support the concept of the bystander effect (less help with others present) and the central idea of the paragraphs.

✓ Practice: Detect the Propaganda Techniques, Misused Words, and Definitions.

1. Identify and label the propaganda techniques. List any words that are used incorrectly (proves, random, average).

    ☞ (1) Extrasensory perception (ESP) is being able to perceive information without using our normal senses. (2) Telepathy is one of the best-known types of ESP. (3) Everyone knows of individuals who have this ability. (4) Carefully controlled experimental research has proven that about ten percent of the population has successfully shown ESP ability. (5) Our federal government should put more money in research into this important area of human behavior.

    a. List the sentence number for each propaganda technique, the propaganda words, and label the type of propaganda.
    sentence   word(s)   label the propaganda technique

    _____

    _____

    _____

    b. Identify by sentence number each word used incorrectly and explain the misuse.
    sentence   word   explain the misuse

    _____

2. Place an "X" by the operational definitions. An operational definition must specify the specific behavior to be observed or state the specific actions of the experimenter.
    ___ a. Hunger is being deprived of food for 24 hours.
    ___ b. Hunger is an unpleasant feeling in the stomach. (Remember the experimenter is the person who must see the behavior.)
    ___ c. Learning is the number of correct answers on this exercise.
    ___ d. Neurotic behavior is behavior that is not so severely abnormal as to require treatment.

3. Place an "X" by the two operational definitions.
   ___ a. Aggression is when a person intends to hurt another.
   ___ b. Aggression is the behavior of the research subject who hits the experimenter after being insulted by the experimenter.
   ___ c. Cognitive dissonance occurs when two conflicting ideas are believed at the same time.
   ___ d. Helping behavior is the behavior of searching through a set of files for a piece of paper without the promise of reward, when asked by a stranger.

4. Circle the eight constructs found in the statements below. Constructs are broad psychological terms, and they do not deal with the sample. For example, female college students in "a." is not a construct.
   a. Female college students who went through a severe initiation experienced cognitive dissonance and liked the group better than similar subjects who went through a mild initiation.
   b. Intelligence is increased by studying geometry.
   c. Punishment causes children to be more pleasant.

5. Circle the seven constructs in the next three sentences.
   a. College students learn more through discussion than through lecture.
   b. Women conform more than men.
   c. Children who are frustrated are more aggressive than children who are not frustrated.

Answers to Practice on Propaganda Techniques and Definitions To get the most benefit from these items, do not read further until you have completed all of the practice

1. Propaganda Techniques and Misused Words
   a. Propaganda techniques: (3) "everyone knows" - bandwagon; (4) "carefully controlled research" - glittering generality, (5) "important area" - glittering generality.
   b. Words used incorrectly: (4) "proven" - Research evidence supports. It doesn't prove.

2. An "X" should have been placed before these letters: a, c.

3. An "X" should have been placed before these letters: b, d.

4. These words should have been circled: "punishment," "more pleasant," "intelligence," "studying geometry," "severe initiation," "cognitive dissonance," "liked the group better," and "mild initiation."

5. These words should have been circled: "learn more," "discussion," "lecture," "conform more," "who are frustrated," "more aggressive," "not frustrated." The word "children" is a characteristic of the sample and not a construct.

➬ 4.1: Exercise in Thinking Critically

Answer the questions about "The Bystander" by Ed Jones (1995) using sentences (5) - (7) which are provided from the article on p. 45. The citation is done for you.

☞   (5) In a second study, Latane and Rodin (1969) had forty male college subjects hear a "lady in distress" in the next room. (6) The female experimenter went into the next room, fell off a chair, and screamed loudly for help (the accident was on tape). (7) Seventy percent of the alone subjects helped, while only twenty percent of the subjects who were in the presence of another helped.

a.   **Citation**
       Researchers -- Latane and Daley
       Year -- 1969
       Sentences -- (5) - (7)
       Related research -- sentences (2) - (4) Latane and Darley, 1968; (8) - (10) Darley and Latane, 1968; (12) Piliavin, Rodin, and Piliavin, 1969.
       Recent research -- There is no research since 1969.

b.   **Subjects**
       Characteristics --

       Number --
       Selection process from the population --

       What is left out? (See p. 41.)

       What problem do you see with the subjects? (See p. 41.)

c.   **Procedure**
       How was the study done?

       Was a control group used?

Were the subjects randomly assigned to groups?

Are the independent and dependent variables precisely defined?

Are other variables controlled?

What are the limited circumstances? (See p. 14.)

Was any important information left out? (See pp. 42-43.)

Are there any problems with the procedure? (See p. 43.)

d.   Results
State the results which can be quoted.

What important information is missing from the results?

What problem do you see with the results?

e.   Reasoning Problems
How does this evidence relate to the key points and central idea? (See pp. 43-44.)

Does the writer draw conclusions not supported by the evidence?

Answers are on pp. 65-66.

❧ 4.2: Exercise in Thinking Critically

Read the following and evaluate the evidence and the reasoning by answering the questions below.

☞   Dr. Shoe (1980) wanted to find out the attitudes of high school students living in Fargo, North Dakota, toward the use of alcohol. He decided to talk with 30 students from each of the eight high schools in the county. He asked 16 college students to help him by having two go to each high school on an afternoon in September, and talk with a random sample of 30 students. The college students talked with the first 30 students who came out of school at the end of the school day. The high school students were asked to state their attitudes toward the use of alcohol and their views about increasing the drinking age. Dr. Shoe found out from his research helpers that most of the students at five of the high schools thought that drinking was OK. Dr. Shoe concluded that teenagers do not see any problems with drinking alcohol.

1.   What is the population that Dr. Shoe wished to study?

2.   Who are the subjects and what are their characteristics?

3.   How big is the sample that was used?

4.   Describe how the sampling was done.

5.   List several problems with the sampling process.

6.   Describe what might be a better approach to get a random sample for this population.

7.   Describe at least two other problems with Dr. Shoe's thinking and research.

Chapter 5
Practice in Thinking Critically
About a Source

Preview Use the four step procedure to evaluate secondary psychological sources.

✓ Practice: Use the Four Steps to Think Critically

Answer the questions that follow the article. This article by Renea Gain is entitled "To Go Or Not To Go To Nursery School" and appeared in *Early Childhood Education Digest*, 1990, Volume 65, pp. 110-111.

☞ (1) Parents of children ages two to four wonder about the value of nursery school. (2) Children from upper class families do not seem to benefit very much from nursery school according to recent psychological research reported in England (Burt, 1978). (3) Several researchers have found that children from very deprived homes show dramatic increases in creativity. (4) Karlins (1972) found that social emotional development was improved by nursery school attendance. (5) Race (1977) found that sixty girls who had attended nursery school were rated by trained observers at the start of first grade as committing less than half as many aggressive acts of hitting in one 30 minute outdoor play session as sixty girls who had not gone to nursery school. (6) Punishment, however, increases aggression (Able, 1944; Best, 1966, Few, 1972).

(7) In my work as a psychologist, I randomly visited two nursery schools in Howard County, Maryland, and found that some of the children were already starting to read. (8) The major reason I would send my child to nursery school is to increase his/her intelligence. (9) Piaget proposed a reasonable theory of intellectual development which indicated that the ages prior to age five are crucial (1943, 1946, 1956, 1970, 1972). (10) Dr. Melton, a nursery school teacher, is firmly convinced of the value of education and has said: "Intellectual development is greatly influenced by attendance at school" (Melton, 1925, p. 12). (11) Miller (1988) measured the intelligence of 100 males and 100 females after attendance for one year at three different types of nursery schools in Baltimore, Maryland. (12) The average IQ on the Stanford-Binet Intelligence Test was 120 for the boys. (13) Boone (1987) reported a Stanford-Binet IQ of 116 for children after two years of nursery school. (14) The research just cited proves that nursery school increases intelligence. (15) Funki (1968) found an IQ of 84 for lower class children after three years in a Head Start nursery school in Washington, D.C.

(16) Research has proven that parents believe nursery school is valuable in increasing intelligence. (17) The most compelling experiment was recently done by Sea (1989) who used 12 identical twins. (18) One member of each set of twins was sent to nursery school, while the other stayed home. (19) The six twins who went to nursery school were tested before going to nursery school. (20) After attending a year of nursery school, their IQs increased on the average by five IQ points. (21) Everyone knows that children should go to nursery school because the benefits gotten there cannot be obtained in any other way.

Write your answers on the lines below and then check your answers.

Step 1: Identify the source.
a.   Who wrote the source? _____
b.   Where was it published? _____
c.   When was it published? _____

Step 2: Read to understand the article.
a.   What is the author's central idea? Identify the sentence or sentences and then put the idea into your own words.

_____

_____

b.   What are the key points? Write the numbers of the relevant sentences.
      Answer given for you: (2), (3), (4), (5), (7), and (14).

c.   List two additional words used incorrectly. Use only sentences (7) - (16).

	sentence	word	explain the misuse
Example	(7)	randomly	does not state how selected

_____

_____

d.   Identify and label four additional propaganda techniques found in sentences (3) - (10), (16) - (21).

	sentence	word(s)	label the propaganda technique
Example	(3)	dramatic increases	glittering generality

_____

_____

_____

_____

Step 3: Identify the research evidence.
Identify the incomplete research evidence and the research evidence by listing the sentence number(s) and the citation. Research evidence may include more than one sentence. Write the numbers of all of the sentences that make up each example of the research evidence. Check the full article.

a.   Incomplete research evidence

	sentence(s)	researcher(s)	year
Example	(2)	Burt	1978

_____

_____

b.   Research evidence

	sentence(s)	researcher	year
Example	(11) - (12)	Miller	1988

_____

_____

Answer Key
Steps 1, 2, and 3

Now that you have thought critically using the first three steps, check your answers.

Step 1: Identifying the source.
    a.   Who wrote the source? *Gain*
    b.   Where was it published? *Early Childhood Education Digest*
    c.   When was it published? *1990*

Step 2: Reading to understand the article.
    a.   What was the author's central idea? Identify the sentence or sentences and then put his idea into your own words.
        (21) Children derive unique benefits from attending nursery school.

    b.   What are the key points? Write the numbers of the sentences.
        (2), (3), (4), (5), (7) and (14)

    c.   List any words used incorrectly.
        (7) randomly (no evidence that a random selection process was used)
        (14) proves (evidence does not prove)
        (16) proof (evidence is not proof in psychology)

    d.   List and identify the propaganda techniques.
        (3) dramatic increases (glittering generality)
        (9) a reasonable theory (glittering generality)
        (10) a doctor and teacher (testimonial)
        (17) the most compelling experiment (glittering generality)
        (21) everyone knows (bandwagon)

Step 3: Identifying the research evidence (the incomplete research evidence and the research evidence).
    a.   Incomplete research evidence
        (2) Burt, 1978
        (4) Karlins, 1972
        (13) Boone, 1987
        (15) Funki, 1968

    b.   Research evidence
        (5) Race, 1977
        (11) - (12) Miller, 1958
        (17) - (20) Sea, 1989

Step 4: See 5.1 Exercise on Thinking Critically.

Key Concepts for Thinking Critically

Nonscientific Evidence (Chapter 4)	Scientific Psychological Evidence (Chapter 2)	
Opinions Value judgements Personal experiences Secondhand reports Unsupported assertions	**Descriptive Evidence** Clinical observations Correlational studies Naturalistic observations Surveys Tests	**Experimental Evidence** Hypothesis Independent variable Dependent variable Controlled variables Random assignment Control group Experimental group Limited circumstances

The Four Steps to Thinking Critically

Step 1: Identify the Source

    a. Who wrote the source? Include all of the authors.
    b. Where was it published? Name the journal, book or newspaper.
    c. When was it published (year)? Is this a recent source?

Step 2: Read to Understand

    a. State in your own words the central idea.
    b. State the key points.
    c. Note instances of the misuse of these words: "proves," "random," "average."
    d. Label any propaganda techniques: bandwagon, extreme statements, glittering generalities, name calling, testimonials.

Step 3: Identify the Research Evidence

Psychological Research Evidence
Citation
Results based on observations
Description of the study
    a. Subjects
    b. Procedure

Incomplete Research Evidence
Citation
Results based on observations
No description of the study

Step 4: Evaluate the Research Evidence

Citation Who did the study? When? List any related research. How recent?
Sample Who was studied? Their characteristics? Number? How selected? What is left out? Are there any problems with the subjects?
Procedure How the study was done? Was there a control group? Random assignment? Were the independent and dependent variables precisely defined? Controlled variables? Limited circumstance? What is left out? Are there problems with the procedure?
Results What was discovered? What is missing? Are there any problems with the results?
Reasoning problems? Are there any reasoning problems? Does the evidence support the key points? Does the author go beyond the evidence?

◆◆ 5.1: Exercise in Thinking Critically, Step 4

Evaluate the second research evidence in lines (11) - (12) by Miller, 1988, from the article on preschool education on page 53.

☞   (11) Miller (1988) measured the intelligence of 100 males and 100 females after attendance for one year at three different types of nursery schools in Baltimore, Maryland. (12) The average IQ on the Stanford-Binet Intelligence Test was 120 for the boys.

a.   Citation
Researcher -- Miller
Year -- 1988
Sentences -- (11) - (12)
Related research -- (13) - (14) Boone, 1987; and (17) - (20) Sea, 1989 are also on intelligence.
Recent research -- The Sea study in 1989 is the most recent.

b.   Subjects
Characteristics --

Number --

Selection process from the population --

What is left out?

What problem do you see with the subjects?

c.   Procedure
How was the study done?

Was a control group used? Were the subjects randomly assigned to groups?

Are the independent and dependent variables precisely defined?

Are other variables controlled?

What are the limited circumstances?

Is any important information left out?

Are there any problems with the procedure?

d. Results
State the results.

What important information is missing from the results?

What problem do you see with the results?

e. Reasoning Problems
How is this evidence related to the key points and central idea?

Does the writer draw conclusions not supported by the evidence?

Answers are on pp. 67-68.

☞ 5.2: Exercise in Thinking Critically, Step 4

Evaluate the third example of research evidence from the article on preschool education on p. 53.

☞   (17) The most compelling experiment was recently done by Sea (1989) who used 12 identical twins. (18) One member of each set of twins was sent to nursery school, while the other stayed home. (19) The six twins who went to nursery school were tested before going to nursery school. (20) After attending a year of nursery school, their IQs increased on the average by five IQ points.

a.   Citation

Researcher -- Sea
Year -- 1989
Sentences -- (17) - (20)
Related research -- (11) - (12), Miller, 1988; and (13) - (14), Boone, 1987.
Recent evidence -- The 1989 study by Sea is the most recent.

b.   Subjects

Characteristics --

Number --

Selection process from the population --

What is left out?

What problem do you see with the subjects?

c.   Procedure

How was the study done?

Was a control group used? Were the subjects randomly assigned to groups?

Are the independent and dependent variables precisely defined?

Are other variables controlled?

What are the limited circumstances?

Is any important information left out?

Are there any problems with the procedure?

d.   Results
State the results.

What important information is missing from the results?

What problem do you see with the results?

e.   Reasoning Problems
How is this evidence related to the key points and central idea?

Does the writer draw conclusions not supported by the evidence?

Chapter 6
Use the Four Steps to Think Critically

Preview You have practiced the 4 steps to think critically about secondary psychological sources. You are not expected to memorize the steps and the accompanying questions, but you need to be able to use each step.

■ Four Steps to Use When Thinking Critically About Secondary Psychological Sources

Use the four steps to think critically about the article "The Dangerous Drugs" which starts on page 63. Turn in 59-62. All errors in the article are deliberate. The article was designed for you to read very carefully and to think critically. Assume that a page of references is provided at the end of the article.

Name: _____   Instructor: _____

Step 1: Identify the source.
a.   Who wrote the article? _____
b.   Where was the article published? _____
c.   When was the article published (year)? _____

Step 2: Read to understand.
a.   Identify by number the sentence or sentences which is (are) the central idea.
      Sentence(s): _____
b.   In a complete sentence, put the central idea into your own words.

      _____

      _____

c.   The key points are listed here for you: Sentences (4), (5), (14), (22)

d.   List three key words or phrases that are used incorrectly and explain. Use the entire article.
      (Words often used incorrectly are proof, random, and average.)

	sentence	word	explain the misuse
1.	_____	_____	_____
2.	_____	_____	_____
3.	_____	_____	_____

e.   Find three different types of propaganda techniques (bandwagon, extreme statements, glittering generalities, name calling, testimonials) and label them. Use the entire article.

	sentence	word(s)	label the type of propaganda technique
1.	_____	_____	_____
2.	_____	_____	_____
3.	_____	_____	_____

Step 3: Identify the research evidence.

a.   Identify three **incomplete research**. Check the entire article.

	sentence(s)	researcher(s)	year
1.	_____	_____	_____
2.	_____	_____	_____
3.	_____	_____	_____

b.   Identify four **research evidence.** Check the entire article.

	sentence(s)	researcher(s)	year
1.	_____	_____	_____
2.	_____	_____	_____
3.	_____	_____	_____
4.	_____	_____	_____

Step 4: Evaluate the research evidence in sentences (9) - (11) by Say (1948).

a.   Citation

1.   Who did the study in sentences (9) - (11)? _____

2.   When was the study published? _____

3.   What related research is described? _____

         _____

4.   How recent is the evidence? _____

         _____

b.   Subjects

1.   Who are the subjects? _____

2.   Describe the characteristics of the subjects. _____

         _____

         _____

3.   How many total subjects are there? _____

4.   How were the subjects selected? _____

         _____

What are two important pieces of information **left out** about the subjects?

1.   _____

         _____

2.   _____

         _____

What is one **problem** with the subjects?

1.   _____

         _____

c.   Procedure What are three pieces of important information **left out** about the procedure? Do not put information about the sample here. Do not summarize how the study was done.

1.   _____

         _____

2.   _____

         _____

3.   _____

         _____

What are two **problems** with the procedure?

1. _____

2. _____

d. Results

Directly quote the **results** using quotation marks.

1. _____

What are two important pieces of information **missing** from the results?

1. _____

2. _____

What is one **problem** with the results?

1. _____

e. Reasoning Problems

1. How is the evidence related to a key point and the central idea?

_____

2. Does the writer draw conclusions not supported by the evidence?

_____

Step 4: Evaluate the research evidence in sentences (27) - (31) by Brite, (1934).

a. Citation

1. Who did the study in sentences (27) - (31)? _____

2. When was the study published? _____

3. What related research is described? _____

4. How recent is the evidence? _____

b. Subjects

1. Who are the subjects? _____

2. Describe the characteristics of the subjects. _____

3. How many total subjects are there? _____

4. How were the subjects selected? _____

What are two important pieces of information **left out** about the subjects?

1. _____

2. _____

What is one **problem** with the subjects?

1. _____

c.   **Procedure** What are three important pieces of information **left out** about the procedure? Do not put information about the sample here. Do not summarize how the study was done.

1. _____

2. _____

3. _____

What are two **problems** with the procedure?

1. _____

2. _____

d.   **Results**

Directly quote the **results** using quotation marks.

1. _____

What are two important pieces of information **missing** from the results?

1. _____

2. _____

What is one **problem** with the results?

1. _____

e.   **Reasoning Problems**

1.   How is the evidence related to a key point and the central idea?

_____

_____

2.   Does the writer draw conclusions not supported by the evidence?

_____

_____

❧ 6.1: Exercise in Thinking Critically

Use the four step procedure to think critically as you study this article. Follow the directions starting on page 59.

"The Dangerous Drugs," by Edward Son, Ph.D. is found in the *Journal of Drug Education*, 1996, volume 6, on page 5. Dr. Son is a psychologist who does research on the influence of marijuana on driving and has written books on the drug problem.

☞ (1) Americans today use many illegal drugs. (2) However, it is the misuse of these drugs, particularly alcohol, marijuana, and cocaine that is causing serious problems. (3) This misuse must be stopped. (4) In the first place, society is harmed by the misuse of drugs. (5) Lower productivity and increased aggressiveness are two ways that society is harmed. (6) In an important study Hat (1972) found that receptionists who were drinkers (alcohol) made more errors than women who did not drink. (7) Additionally, recent important research demonstrated conclusively that car workers high on marijuana produce less than other car workers. (8) Bart (1981) studied 1800 female high school typists who did poorer work after having some marijuana. (9) Say (1958) found that women who smoked had slower reading speeds. (10) Thirty-four young women randomly selected were given a standard reading test, asked to smoke, and then given the same test again. (11) Twenty of the women read slower while only six read at the same rate or faster. (12) Making more errors, producing less, doing poorer work, and reading slower are all ways that America's productivity is damaged by the misuse of illegal drugs. (13) Everyone has heard how society is harmed by the poor quality of America's low productivity.

(14) Society has to pay the cost of increased aggressiveness because of increases in crime due to the misuse of hard drugs. (15) Aggressiveness is that behavior which is intended to do harm to others (Berkowitz, 1980, *Dictionary of Psychology*, page 12). (16) Cocaine users are verbally more aggressive when angry than non-cocaine users, according to one very recent Harvard University study. (17) Most fans are aware that football players use drugs to make themselves more aggressive. (18) Pack (1973) fed marijuana to rats who bit more often than mice who ate no marijuana. (19) The rats had been randomly placed into the two groups by flipping a coin. (20) "It is a well-established fact that great evil and crime are done by the addicts who kill and rob while drunk," said Dr. Pert, an authority on the subject. (21) Any objective observer can see that society cannot continue to pay the high cost of both lower productivity and increased aggressiveness.

(22) Not only is society seriously harmed, but also there are great dangers to the drug user. (23) Extensive research shows that alcohol dulls human critical thinking. (24) For example, Sands (1955) found that bright dogs were slower at making a correct decision after having drunk alcohol than identical dogs who drank water. (25) More and more young people are ruining their lives with drugs as demonstrated by youngsters jumping off roofs while high on LSD, and others are going blind while staring at the sun (Fool, *The New York Times*, April 30, 1976, page B4). (26) Reliable government statistics have proven that using marijuana leads to slower reflexes which causes injuries to drivers. (27) Brite (1934) randomly selected 80 college freshmen from a general psychology class at the University of Maryland. (28) The 40 who had smoked marijuana previously were given five joints each to smoke. (29) Each man was then given an individual intelligence test. (30) The men who smoked the five joints did not do as well on the IQ test (three I.Q. points lower on the

average) or on a creativity test as the 40 men who had not previously used marijuana and were given three joints. (31) This research proves that marijuana smoking decreases intelligence in a harmful way. (32) Ride and Park (1966) individually interviewed 600 randomly selected high school seniors from all eight high schools in Howard County, Maryland (70 per school). (33) Those women who individually reported a D grade point average to trained high school interviewers were not as likely to have tried cocaine as women reporting an A average. (34) These five experiments demonstrate conclusively that permanent damage is done when using hard drugs. (35) Psychologists have also studied the effects on creativity. (36) Dreary and Leary (1990) found that LSD decreased creativity. (37) They gave each of nine hard fiction writers a small bit of pure LSD. (38) Each writer was asked to write a story based on "Mary Had A Little Lamb." (39) All but five produced highly unusual stories compared to their efforts before being told to take the LSD. (40) A second story was later used and they got almost the same results. (41) Since society is harmed and the drug user is exposed to great dangers, the time has come to stop this devastating menace.

Check your work to see that you have fully evaluated the article.

Congratulations on completing this book on critical thinking. Becoming an effective critical thinker is not easy. On page 72 is an organized list of the key questions which can serve as a guide to help you when reading psychological topics.

I collect extensive feedback from my students at Howard Community College and would like to hear from you. My e-mail address is rjbell@erols.com.

Appendix

Answer Key for 1.1: Exercise in Thinking Critically p. 8

Statements 2, 3, and 6 are "C."   9 is "I."   1, 4, 5, 7, 8, and 10 are "?".

Answer Key for 2.1: Exercise in Thinking Critically p. 22

1. List all of the citations. List the sentence, author, and year.
    Example: (3) Festinger, 1957 (indicates when the book was published)
                  (5) Aronson, 1968. (A statement about the theory.)
                  (8) Festinger and Carlsmith, 1959
                  (14) Aronson and Carlsmith, 1963
                  (17) Freedman, 1965
                  (20) Soronson, 1989 (indicates an opinion)

2. List the sentences that contain research evidence and the citation.
    (8) - (13) Festinger and Carlsmith, 1959. Be sure to include the description of the study and the research results sentences.
    (14) Aronson and Carlsmith, 1963. Here all the information is found in one sentence.
    (17) - (19) Freedman, 1965. (Citation, description, results)

Answer Key for 3.1: Exercise in Thinking Critically p. 31

1. Read to understand.
    a. Central idea -- Preschool education is very valuable for children. Sentence 1.
    b. Words used incorrectly -- (3) proves. Evidence in psychology does not prove. (4) average children. It is not clear which meaning of average is being used.
    c. Propaganda techniques -- (4) highly significant research - glittering generality; (4) clearly demonstrates - glittering generality; (5) famous Swiss psychologist - testimonial

2. Label the propaganda techniques.
    a   Bandwagon
    b. Testimonial
    c. Glittering generality
    d. Name calling
    e. Extreme Statement

Answer Key for 4.1: Exercise in Thinking Critically pp. 49-50

a. **Citation**
    Researchers -- Latane and Darley
    Year -- 1969
    Sentences -- (5) - (7)
    Related research -- Latane and Darley, 1968, (2) - (4); Darley and Latane, 1968, (8) - (10);   Piliavin, Rodin, and Piliavin, 1969, (12)
    How recent? -- The most recent research is 1989. Is there more recent research?

b. Subjects

Characteristics -- Male college students were the subjects.

Number -- 40 total

Selection process from the population -- No information is given.

What is left out? -- No information is given about their age, about other characteristics, or how they were selected. Don't know how many subjects were in each group?

Problems with the subjects -- It is not clear what population the students represented since it is not clear if random sampling was used.

c. Procedure

How was the study done? -- A women, the experimenter in the study, fell off of a chair in the next room, and screamed loudly for help.

Was a control group used? Yes. Were the subjects randomly assigned to groups? -- There is no information about how subjects were placed into the two groups of different sizes, one or two persons.

Are the variables precisely defined? -- The size of the groups is precise: 1 or 2. Exactly what help was given was not defined.

Are other variables controlled? -- The fall and call for help were on tape (assume that it was an audio only tape) and so were held constant for all subjects. The length of the scream and what she said was controlled but not defined. Was the women a stranger to the subjects? Could the women be seen? Don't know about other variables.

What are the limited circumstances? -- Experimenter (female) with male subjects, accident of falling from a chair and calling for help, could not see the women (?), was the help just letting someone else know? Or going into the room to help? Or what?

What important information was left out? -- What were the subjects doing prior to the accident? How much interaction was there with the experimenter? Did subjects later report they were clear that it was an accident?

What problems are there with the procedure? -- If subjects were not randomly assigned to groups, we don't know that the groups were equal to start with. The study needed some larger groups to see if the bystander hypothesis held at larger sizes.

d. Results

State the results -- "70% of the alone subjects helped, while only 20% of the subjects were in the presence of another helped."

What is missing? -- How was help, the dependent variable, measured?

What problems do you see with the results? -- None.

e. Reasoning

How does the evidence relate to the key points and central idea? -- Bystanders in groups are less likely to help than individuals in the laboratory. This study provided support for the hypothesis. Stronger support would have involved using larger groups. There is no explanation of why fewer helped when others were around.

Does the writer draw conclusions not supported by the evidence? -- The writer draws reasonable conclusions consistent with the research.

Answer Key for 5.1: Exercise in Thinking Critically pp. 59-60

Step 4: Evaluating the research evidence found in the Miller (1988) study

a. Citation

Researchers -- Miller
Year -- 1988
Sentences -- (11) - (12)
Related research -- Boone, 1987 (13) - (14) Sea, 1989 (17) - (20)
How recent? -- The most recent research is 1989. Is there more recent research?

b. Subjects

Characteristics -- Boys and girls who had completed one year of nursery school were studied from three different types of nursery schools (not specified) in Baltimore, MD. We don't know anything else about the children. For instance, we don't know if they were the same age or represented all social classes.

Number -- 100 males and 100 females

Selection process from the population -- Were the three school selected randomly from all the nursery schools in Baltimore? We don't know how the three nursery schools were chosen. Were the children selected randomly from the schools? We don't know how the 200 children were selected from the nursery schools. Were the three schools equal in size?

What is left out? -- Were the children the same age? Did the children represent all social classes? What population do the children represent?

Problems with the subjects -- It is not clear what population the children represented since it is not clear if random sampling was used with schools and children in schools.

c. Procedure

How was the study done? -- The Stanford-Binet Intelligence Test was given to all 200 children. Since it is an individual test rather than a group test, I assume it was given to children individually. It is not clear if the test was given during the summer after school, at the end of the year, or at the start of the next school year.

Was a control group used? Were the subjects randomly assigned to groups? -- There was no control group.

Are the variables precisely defined? -- "Attendance for one year ... of nursery school" is not precisely defined. Did all of the children have to attend a certain number of days to be used or could a child who had missed half of the year due to illness still be studied? The Stanford Binet IQ test does measure intelligence which is the behavior being measured.

Are other variables controlled? -- No controlled variables were mentioned. Was the curriculum at the schools the same? What type of curriculum was it? Were the children all tested at the same time? No tests were given before nursery school to determine if there was an increase in intelligence. No control group of children were used who did not go to nursery school.

What are the limited circumstances? -- The limited circumstances which are most important are the use of three nursery schools with no explanation as to why these three were used. Limited circumstances of all going to school in Baltimore.

What important information was left out? -- Precise definition of attendance for one year at nursery school. Were all given the tests at the same time? No information is given about the testing circumstances.

What problems are there with the procedure? -- Sentences 10 and 16 suggest that an increase in intelligence from going to nursery school is the key point that this study is relevant to. To conclude that there is an increase means that there must be a control group that did not go to nursery school and that intelligence for both groups must be measured before nursery school. There was no control group in this study and apparently no measurement of IQ before the year of preschool.

d. Results

State the results -- The boys scored an average of 120 on the IQ test which is above the average IQ of 100.

What is missing? -- No information about their scores before nursery school. Is the average score of 120 the mean? median? or mode? No information is given about how the girls scored.

What problems do you see with the results? -- It is hard to interpret the score of 120 for males since we don't know their score before nursery school. No conclusion can be draw about the girls since their results were not given.

e. Reasoning

How does the evidence relate to the key points and central idea? -- The key point deals with intelligence and this study deals with intelligence.

Does the writer draw conclusions not supported by the evidence? -- The writer is trying to convince us that attendance at nursery school is valuable. The longest part of the article is trying to convince us that intelligence is increased by attendance at nursery school. The Miller (1988) study provides us with a mean IQ score of 120 for males which is above the average of 100. However, to show that nursery school increased intelligence, we would need to have scores for these students before they attended nursery school and for a comparison group that did not attend nursery school. The author goes beyond his evidence.

The writer personally believes that the main reason for sending a child to nursery school is to increase intelligence. I believe that learning to cooperate and follow directions, developing persistence, and having fun are more valuable than a stress on increasing intelligence.

References

Aronson, E. (1988). *The social animal.* NY: W. H. Freeman and Company.

Best, J. (1985). The myth of the Halloween sadist. *Psychology Today*, pp. 14-16.

Crossed, C. (1994). *Tainted truth: The manipulation of fact in America.* NY: Simon and Schuster.

Latane, B., & Darley, J. (1969). A lady in distress. *Journal of Experimental Social Psychology, V*, 189-202.

Schiraldi, V. (1998, January 11). The latest trend in juvenile crime: Exaggeration by the news media. *The Washington Post*, p. C5.

Charts

Index

Listed below are the terms discussed in this book. An * indicates those terms which are defined on the next page.

Glossary of Selected Terms

Definitions for the terms used in this book can be found in the glossary of your textbook. The glossary is found at the end of the book. The terms discussed below are usually not found in psychology textbooks' glossaries.

Central idea -- The central idea of a communication, the most important idea the writer is trying to get across, is sometimes called the main point, thesis, purpose or conclusion. The central idea is generally the broadest idea the writers is trying to explain.

Citation -- The word "citation" in psychology has two different meanings. Citation is used to identify a source that is being studied. For example, what is the citation for your textbook? Within your textbook your authors refer to psychological studies. Each of these studies is identified by a citation. Consequently, citation can (1) identify the whole source, or (2) identify the researchers within the source.

Evidence -- Evidence is the information used to decide which statements to believe. The focus of this book is on evaluating the scientific research evidence found in secondary sources. Some writers use the term "proof" or "proves." Proof is a word used in math but not in psychology. Evidence either supports a hypothesis or helps reject the hypothesis. Evidence does not prove a hypothesis. Another caution about psychological research is the idea of limited circumstances. All psychological research is conducted in a particular place with a specific independent variable, a set of controlled variables, and a specific dependent variable. The results from any one study may not apply in different circumstances. The concept of limited circumstances means that all psychological research, not just experiments, occur in specific circumstances and may not be accurate in other circumstances.

Key points -- Ideas that relate to the central idea are the key points. Check to determine if the key points are supported by scientific or nonscientific evidence. Evaluate the evidence that supports or does not support the key points.

Propaganda techniques -- There are many different ways to mislead readers. Logic textbooks and critical thinking textbooks explain a large variety of propaganda techniques. Five major techniques are described in this book.

Questions to Use When Thinking Critically About a Secondary Source in Psychology

Step 1: Identify the Source.
   a. Who wrote the source?
   b. Where was it published?
   c. When was it published (year)?

Step 2: Read to Understand.
   a. What is the author's central idea?
   b. What are the key points?
   c. Are any words used incorrectly ("proves," "random," "average")?
   d. List and label the propaganda techniques (bandwagon, extreme statements, glittering generalities, name calling, testimonial).

Step 3: Identify the Research Evidence.
   a. Identify the incomplete research evidence.
   b. Identify the research evidence.

Step 4: Evaluate the Research Evidence.
   a. Citation
       Who did the study and when? Is related research given? Is the research recent?

   b. Subjects
       Characteristics? Number? Selection process used? What is left out? What problems are there with the subjects?

   c. Procedure
       How was the study done? Was there a control group? Were the subjects randomly assigned to groups? Are the independent and dependent variables precisely defined? What variables are controlled? What are the limited circumstances? What important information is left out? What problems are there with the procedure?

   d. Results
       What was discovered? What important information is missing from the results? What problems are there with the results?

   e. Reasoning Problems
       Are there any reasoning problems? Does the evidence support the key points? Does the author draw conclusions that go beyond the evidence?